Self in Relation

PETER PHILIPPSON

Self in Relation

With a Foreword by Philip Lichtenberg, Ph.D.

A Publication of
The Gestalt Journal Press

ISBN 0-939266-40-7

ISBN 978-0-939266-40-7

CONTENTS

FOREWORD

The special nature of this book, which should make it attractive to Gestalt therapists, is that it puts forward the developed perspective of a bright and thoughtful contributor to ongoing debates in the theoretical waters. It is seriously indebted to the original writings of *Gestalt Therapy*, the book by Perls, Hefferline, and Goodman and original works by Frederick Perls, and is not intended to replace those texts or consign them to the backwaters. Yet it is not a basic introduction to the theory in the traditions of Erving and Miriam Polster or Joel Latner. Nor is it an extended singular argument on some aspect of the conceptual foundations of Gestalt therapy, though it veers in that direction with its attention to the concept of "field" and the ramifications of a field approach. Rather, it is one person's reading of the theory and of developments in recent years around that theory.

Here is the author's way of saying what the book purports to be. "I [am] presenting here my own map of Gestalt therapy, from its first principles in philosophy to its expression in specific methods of psychotherapy. This . . . is particularly geared to the Gestalt therapist, who wishes to get a sense of where I stand on various aspects of Gestalt theory. I am also keen to encourage others to make their own 'maps' and show how the theory hangs together for them" (p. 217).

The author's map covers a broad territory. He addresses the differentiation of Gestalt therapy from constructivism and Humanistic Psychology; a relational view of self; field in contradistinction to system; the pulsation of undifferentiated conditions moving into stable structures; predictability and complexity; creative adjustment; interruptions in contacting; sexual abuse; dialogue; and group nature and process among various other topics. His range of interests is broad.

Every theoretician writes from his or her experience, and, therefore, from his or her bias. The tilt in the author's perspective, I believe, is toward a strong construction of self in relation. His view is much like that of Frederick Perls and approaches Perls' personal style. This orientation shows most clearly in his analysis of dialogue, his view of field, his thinking on groups, and his clinical use of self in dealing with clients. He eschews empathic attunement, a giving over of the therapist's separateness in the effort to merge with the client. To promote effective dialogue, he makes himself a strong "other" with whom the client is entreated to engage, sometimes by his being an attractive or curious other, and sometimes a frustrating other when the client wants confluence too soon or too arbitrarily.

His focus on field entails the dialectic of chaos, disorder, unpredictability with ordering, stabilizing, regularity. Heightening both sides in this drama is the strategy that follows upon his special bias. Thus, in his attention to groups, he favors a "street" conception, which allows for the disorderliness of anonymous life in the city moving into patterns and dances of relationship. His particular rendering of interruptions to contact — too ecumenical for my taste — follows as well along the lines of this dialectic.

His discussions of how he works clinically, including his composite case descriptions, show him to be adept at holding to being a vivid, direct, unique individual posing challenges to his clients. They, in turn, are asked to create their own self forms and they are required to connect with his clear articulation of himself as a separate other. If there is a favoring of individuality over community, it is a slight difference, and the resultant is a rich person and a potentially profound, if temporary, community.

Gestalt therapists will benefit significantly when they read this book, agree and disagree with its arguments, and discover in the process their own predilections and tendencies. Maybe their own "map" will become clearer. In any case, they will find it well worth the effort they put into it.

Philip Lichtenberg
Bryn Mawr, Pennsylvania
June 30, 2001

ACKNOWLEDGMENTS

This book arises from a rich field of those who have influenced my own Gestalt development, people who have supported and challenged me. I would like to name some (but by no means all) of those people. This does not of course imply that they would agree with all my conclusions.

I want to begin by acknowledging Petruska Clarkson, my primary trainer, who took me into Gestalt training as a burnt-out philosopher wanting to stop thinking and start feeling, and showed me by her example and encouragement that I could both think *and* feel! I also appreciate the way she supported me in finding my own approach to Gestalt therapy, and accepted that my way would be different to her way.

My love and gratitude goes to John Bernard Harris, a co-founder of Manchester Gestalt Centre and another ex-philosopher. We have worked together since 1985, and have provided each other with a sounding board for our ideas and theories, which we have then tried out in practice with the long-suffering members of the therapy group we run together. He also provided support in reading the manuscript and providing detailed comments.

I have also been supported by the other members of Manchester Gestalt Centre: Shirley and Graeme Summers, and Elizabeth Jackson.

During the course of my thinking and writing, I have corresponded with a number of Gestaltists, and I would like to name two of these in particular. Hunter Beaumont's thinking about 'fragile self process' has been a strong influence, as has his fearless honesty with clients. Gary Yontef is tremendously generous in his feedback to myself and other Gestaltists who write on theory. I have been inspired by his understanding and support of basic Gestalt therapy theory, coupled with his willingness to integrate ideas from other approaches without ever diluting the basics.

Thanks also to Joe Wysong at the Gestalt Journal Press for his support and encouragement for this book.

It seems right to mention here Ernest Rossi, Jungian analyst, Ericksonian hypnotherapist and psychobiology researcher (and an early participant in therapy groups with Frederick Perls), whose 'minimalist' approach to hypnotherapy has influenced my work in ways I find difficult to put into words.

I would like to thank the clients whose writing I have included in the book, as well as all the other clients who have accompanied me on my journey of rediscovery of Gestalt therapy.

Last, but not least, I would like to lovingly acknowledge my wife Mary and my sons Jeffrey and Robert, who kept my feet on the ground while my head was in the air, and (mostly) tolerated my preoccupation with this book over four years. I did much of my reading on infant development in the company of my own infant, which added a whole extra dimension to the subject. Mary provided her own knowledge as a doctor (and Medical Director of Manchester Gestalt Centre), as well as her caring and support.

Peter Philippson
December, 1999

Chapter 1

INTRODUCTION — WHO AM I?

One of the distinguishing features for human beings is the ability to ask questions concerning our own existence: "Who and what am I?", "How do I know things?", "Is there a meaning behind my life?", "Did someone make us?", "What is life?" Our answers have been variously religious, philosophical, cultural and scientific. In the name of our different answers, we have waged holy wars, lived lives of happiness and torment, and found other human beings to be soulmates or enemies, or incomprehensible. We have taken apart the fabric of life and matter and risked our annihilation in the quest to find answers.

This is a book about 'self,' one which takes a particular perspective. I will summarize this here by saying that the experience on which I base the concept of 'self,' and by which our self-experience changes, is my varied contacts with the world I live in, with *otherness*, rather than 'inner' experiencing. To put it simply, I experience myself as the one who sees the sunlight coming through the window, who loves my family, who types on the computer. My focus is on the window, the family, or the computer, not on the seeing, the loving, or my wanting to type. As I move from the computer to my son, my self-experience changes, as does his.

When self is thought about in this way, its primary characteristics are fluidity and relationship. Whereas an 'inner' self, characterized by stability and independence, raises questions of "How does self change?" and "How does self relate to the world?" relational self raises the question "How does self stabilize itself?"

The people who have thought most about issues to do with selfhood are philosophers, religious people, and psychotherapists or counselors of varying approaches. This book attempts the difficult job of coming from two of these perspectives: philosophy and psychotherapy. My hope is that those primarily interested in the therapeutic aspects of the Gestalt approach will find the philosophy interesting and clarifying in regard to what we are doing in therapy; and that those primarily interested in the philosophy will find this clarified by the discussion of the therapeutic implications.

I have put at the end of the book (Chapter 14) what I call a 'map' of Gestalt therapy. I find such maps, charting the interrelationship between different concepts (for example, dialogue, experiment, figure-ground, awareness) important to prevent the therapy from becoming a fragmented 'toolkit.' Those already interested in Gestalt therapy might find it useful to read this chapter first as a concise overview of my approach to therapy. It is, however, a simplification of the viewpoint that I develop in the book.

A QUICK AND NAIVE OVERVIEW OF PHILOSOPHIES OF SELF

Philosophers have taken various approaches to the self. Plato regarded the self as the 'essence' of the person with a separate existence to the physical person, in the same way as he believed the essence of 'redness' has a separate existence from an individual red ball. This approach can be called 'dualism,' as there are two forms of existence: self/mind/spirit and physical bodies.

This can appear a simple answer to the problem, and it has been taken up, explicitly or implicitly, by 'common-sense' understanding and by various religious creeds. The complexity comes when you ask the question "How does mind affect the body?" The approach in this book tries to hold to a non-dualistic understanding of self, without going to the other pole of reductionism (see below).

Descartes also gave a separate existence to the mind/self, and in fact he saw its existence as even more sure than that of the physical world. For what I see of the physical world can be an illusion, but even in my doubting I affirm my existence: "I think therefore I am." Unfortunately, this is a circular piece of reasoning, starting off with the assumption that there is an agent ('I') to do the thinking or doubting and then using that assumption to prove the agent's existence. (We shall later come to a different kind of circularity, which works better.)

Hume saw the 'I' as existing only in the stream of experiences. We cannot be aware directly of any separate self having these experiences. This would be supported by Gestalt therapy.

Existentialist philosophers (for example, Sartre and Kierkegaard) wanted to get away from the dualism of Plato, and they emphasized the primacy of the experiences of living and dying. This emphasis on experience is one of the foundations of Gestalt therapy.

Reductionist philosophers understand 'mind' and 'self' as being physiological brain events, which have their own character, but ones which will be best understood by understanding the brain better. The assumption, which I do not share, is that the rules for higher-complexity processes such as awareness can be derived from the rules for more basic processes such as the chemistry of neurotransmitters. I show below that modern science does not think like this.

Eastern thinkers (for example, Lao Tse and Gautama Buddha) regard the 'ego' as an illusion that causes only suffering. By meditation, we can move beyond the ego. There are strong influences from these philosophies in the Gestalt approach.

The practical philosophers called psychotherapists are also faced with questions about the self. "How does someone come to be the person he is?" "What is psychological health or sickness, and how do they come about?" "What is required from the therapist to bring a client to health, or to experience themselves in a different way?"

Freud and the psychoanalysts see the self as a growing structure within a person through a sequence of developmental steps, which can be disrupted by bad parenting. Freud's aim was to discover and interpret back to the patient how this had happened. Psychoanalytic researchers, in particular Mahler, worked to find the precise developmental steps involved, and the implications of these steps not being completed. Some neo-Freudians such as Reich want rather to restore the fully functioning self by working with the physical process of the disruption. Others such as Kohut want the therapist to provide the parenting experiences which the client never had. Jung emphasizes the individual's emergence from, and connection to, the myths and processes of humanity as a whole. Analytic therapies share with Gestalt therapy an emphasis on exploration rather than the fixing of a 'problem.' However, Gestalt therapy as I understand it, does not look for solutions in the past or in regression.

Behaviourists (for example, Skinner) understand the activity of the self as being merely reflexive responses to stimuli. They want to avoid dealing with 'metaphysical' concepts, and understand the role of the therapist as providing stimuli which research has shown to produce the required response. There are actually very few strict behaviourists these days. Gestalt therapy shares with behaviourist approaches an emphasis on the observable behavior of the client, but without claiming that this is all there is.

Humanistic therapists (for example, Maslow) tread an uneasy path of defining therapy as the rediscovery of a 'real (inner) self,' and yet not becoming full dualists. However, they share with Gestalt therapy an emphasis on the face-to-face relationship between therapist and client.

Some psychiatrists follow the reductionist model and believe the best way to affect self-functioning is by treating problems as physical ones involving neurotransmitters, and therefore amenable to medication. Other psychiatrists are more open to psychotherapy as an adjunct to medical treatment.

MODERN SCIENCE

Philosophers, psychotherapists and religious thinkers all now find ourselves in a strange situation. In humanity's delving into the structure of matter, what appeared to be simple and solid has become increasingly complex and esoteric. Through the scientific theories of relativity and quantum theory, concepts inextricably linked with our commonsense understanding of selfhood such as those of space, time and matter have ceased to have their commonsense meaning. If all matter can be viewed as a probability wave, with each 'particle' having potential connections to other 'particles' which may be vastly distant from it in space and time, a simple equation of "me is inside my skin, not-me is outside" becomes somehow less satisfying.

The central image which I believe comes out of these theories is of solidity arising out of interaction. I am not, as it were, parachuted into a pre-existing solid world. Rather, my interaction influences how the world becomes as solid round me. Furthermore, this is a two-way street. The interaction happens both ways and, from the perspective of my environment, I become solid through my interaction with it. The scientific word for this process is emergence, and emergence is an underlying theme of this book. An emergent reality is compatible with the rules of the context from which it emerges (for example, neurobiology), but also develops its own processes (book writing), which are not derivable from those rules. In the same way, my selfhood arises out of my physical contact with my physical environment, in a way which does not violate the physical rules of that contact (I can't walk through walls), but which also has its own psychological processes which can't be reduced to physics (e.g. commitment and choice).

Psychotherapy also has to find a way to come to terms with emergence. What does it mean to work therapeutically with an emergent self in an emergent world? Potentially, this is an exciting question, since it turns more orthodox approaches on their heads. Rather than focusing on change, we can focus on what interactions maintain the solidity of a particular self, even when that way of being oneself has destructive consequences. The therapist is then not strictly a 'change agent' (with all the power dynamics inherent in this), but a co-explorer who helps the client discover where she will and will not explore. From this approach, we would expect a great capacity for change, while the hard work is to account for our sense of ongoing selfhood. This book is written from the perspective of Gestalt therapy, which has taken on this task. I am going to attempt to walk the tightrope between philosophy and psychotherapy, and show how the philosophical approach of Gestalt therapy leads to ways of working whereby change is a constant possibility.

Before going on to look at how Gestalt therapy deals with these questions, I would like to take a detour, and sketch how other approaches have dealt with them, or more often put them aside. My hope is that this will make it easier to understand what I (and Gestalt therapy) am saying.

In the face of the conceptual revolution with which modern science faces us, many have responded by stopping asking the difficult questions. In mathematics, the formalists are interested purely in the formal properties of axiomatic systems, rather than any application to the world. In psychology, the pure behaviourists treat people as what scientists call 'black boxes.' They are not interested in what is going on 'inside,' but in altering external behavior. The orthodox Freudian analysts, on the other hand, treat the outside world as relatively unimportant compared with the inner drama of psychic forces. Finally, 'constructivist' therapies such as Neuro-Linguistic Programming (NLP) see the world as essentially our construct, which we can change at will by viewing it differently.

These approaches have, formally, something in common: whatever events occur, occur within the system. You put in A and

B comes out. How B is derived from A is determined by the system. A is often said to cause B. For the formalist, the axioms cause the theorems. For the behaviourist, the stimulus causes the response. For the analyst, the trauma causes the neurosis. In none of these is there a place for feedback. There is no dialogue, no negotiation between, say, the axioms and the theorems. Stimuli and responses are seen as occurring in chains, not in circles.

And yet, throughout our experience, feedback is one of the central realities. Whether talking to a friend or riding a bicycle my actions are continually informed by the responses of my friend or the bicycle or the road. In fact, it is even less linear than that. There is no separation in real systems between acting and being acted upon: a fact that has been known since Newton's Second Law — "Every action produces an equal and opposite reaction."

THE DANGERS OF A CONSTRUCTIVIST APPROACH

"What shall it profit a man, if he shall gain the whole world, and lose his own soul." (St. Mark, Ch. 8, V. 24)

For the constructivist, our stories about the world cause that world to come into being. Feedback exists in constructivist theories, but with a subtle twist: the aim is usually to control our environment rather than to dialogue with it.

I am going to particular lengths to differentiate the Gestalt theory I am presenting from constructivist theories, particularly Neuro-Linguistic Programming (NLP), since it is comparatively simple to slide from one to the other.* The image I have here is of Gestalt walking along a conceptual tightrope where it is very easy to overbalance in a number of different directions. Then we fail to

---

*A number of Gestaltists (notably Richard Bandler, the co-founder of NLP, Barry Stevens and John Stevens) have made the switch. The formation of NLP was influenced by observing Fritz Perls, as well as Virginia Satir, who herself was influenced by Gestalt. Bandler was the editor of one of Perls' last books (Perls (1976)).

notice that all the words have changed sense, so that what seems like the same sentence now means something totally different.

The meaning of a communication is the effect it has.

This statement, which comes from an NLP handout, for me encapsulates the constructivist view of feedback. In this view no communication takes place in a vacuum. How one communicates something will affect what the response will be. I can get to know what the likely effect of communicating in a number of different ways. How I choose to present my communication — whether in such a way as to get what I want or so as to be more likely not to get it — is part of the meaning of the communication.

Superficially, this looks both reasonable and in line with the relational emphasis which I will be presenting here. However, what is happening here is that I am extending my selfhood and sense of agency into other people. A good example of this occurs in hypnosis, where the 'subject' gives up his or her barriers to being influenced by the 'operator.' There is a great deal of explicit crossover between NLP and hypnosis. The reader can judge for himself the ethics of extending the influence of the hypnotist to everyday interactions. My position is clear: I don't like it.

Let us now turn to the other side of this equation: the effect on the 'operator.' For the person who introjects or becomes confluent with another in order to exert control is also himself controlled by the requirements of that control and that introjection. (Hence my earlier biblical quote.) I believe that the mind-set required by this wish for control is insidious and destructive. It feeds on insecurity and at the same time enhances that insecurity by making true contact impossible. It is the move from the Gestalt position that if I am in good contact with my environment, I am more likely to achieve my wants and needs, to the position that the achievement of these wants and needs takes precedence over the making of contact.

Strangely, we are back to a quite extreme form of emotional repression, but now emotions are replaced by pseudo-emotions rather than overt self-control.

HUMANISTIC PSYCHOLOGY

Another major strand of psychological thinking is the field of humanistic psychology, a diverse field with which Gestalt therapy is often linked. Certainly, both emphasize an *holistic* approach, where mind and body are seen as aspects of one reality. Yet there are important differences, which I would centrally locate in their referencing and understanding of the term *self-actualization.*

This term was initially coined by Kurt Goldstein, a doctor working with brain-damaged soldiers in Germany, who was strongly influenced by the gestalt psychologists. Interestingly, his laboratory assistant was a young German doctor called Fritz Perls, who went on to co-found Gestalt therapy. What Goldstein meant by *self-actualization* was precisely the creation of selfhood out of interaction. As such, it is a descriptive term, talking about what happens.

The term was taken over by one of the founding fathers of humanistic psychology, Abraham Maslow, but with a changed meaning. Now it is a *goal*, a finding of the 'real self.' Maslow (1968) talks about "self-actualizing people," who "devote their lives to the search for what I have called the 'being' values." It is a higher, more spiritual existence, and those who come to this state are morally better as well as happier than those who are not 'self-actualized.' Thus humanistic psychology points towards a spiritual goal with describable consequences, whereas Gestalt therapy explores the actualization inherent in the self that is emerging in the present moment. I shall say more later about how there is an understanding of 'real' and 'false' self in Gestalt; suffice it to say now that this is not described in terms of spiritual advancement or moral improvement.

EMERGENCE

At the beginning of this introduction I talked about the huge shift that modern physical theories have made in how we conceptualize the world. This shift does not lie easily with our ordinary ways of seeing the world. For instance we describe properties as **belonging** to objects and this is reflected in the English language in which adjectives describe the noun. When we say "The ball is green," green-ness is seen as a property of the ball.

Yet modern science is now focusing on **emergent** properties: the properties emerge from a **relationship**. In relativity, space and time have no absolute meaning, but emerge from the relative motion of observer and observed. At molecular, sub-molecular and quantum level, discrete macroscopic "objects" do not exist. Electrons interchange.

On this view, all that exists, all life and matter, is continual interchange. I eat, breathe, defecate, grow, sweat. On a physical level, I am part of an holistic universe, not separated by any real boundary. On a quantum level, things are even more complicated. The physicist David Peat (1994) says:

"Quantum physics pictures the material world as being the outward manifestation of patterns (*i.e. gestalten*), forms, balances, and relations of energy."

Matter/particles are also waves, depending on how they are measured. In quantum physics, matter itself emerges from a field of probabilities in interaction with the observer. 'Green' is a light wavelength in interaction with our eyes and brain. The same 'wave packet' could be measured by other instruments as particles which exert pressure as they collide with the observing apparatus. The green ball changes color as we accelerate away from it. In the retin-ex theory of color vision (Land,1977), particular colors are only visible in relation to the whole visual field, so that green looks green in a variety of lighting conditions.

So this book is an attempt to go with rather than against this scientific trend, and look at this 'thing' called 'self' as a

relational entity, rather than a 'thing in me.' My starting basis is the theory of Gestalt therapy, as outlined in Perls, Hefferline and Goodman: *Gestalt Therapy: Excitement and Growth in the Human Personality.* (I shall call this book 'PHG'). Some of the showier outcrops of this therapy can obscure the fact that Part 2 (Part 1 in the latest edition) of this work is a pioneering work on the philosophy of the self. The concepts are exciting in themselves, and also lend themselves to an extremely exciting and effective psychotherapy.

Of particular interest to me is the profound and subtle way in which Gestalt acknowledges that we filter the world through our perception, and yet stops well short of constructivism, which, as I have argued, is a very destructive philosophy. While this is a book about Gestalt therapy, it is also a book about the emergence of life, and human life in particular, from the complexity of the universe. It is a tribute to the early Gestaltists — Fritz and Laura Perls, Paul Goodman and Paul Weiss — that these two themes can coexist and support each other so easily. My hope is that both therapists and philosophers will find much that will interest them, and feel free to ignore that which does not.

In places in this book there are suggestions for experiments in awareness, which will hopefully illustrate the theory. There are also episodes from work with a client: the client is fictional, but the interactions are ones I encounter frequently in my therapy work. The client could thus be seen to be a composite of a large number of people. I also include a more speculative chapter on the early self-development of this client, which I hope will further give body to the theory. I also include as appendices (with permission) some writing from two clients giving some flavor of how such a therapy appears from their perspectives.

Chapter 2

THE FIELD

. . . We speak of the organism contacting the environment, but it is the contact that is the simplest and first reality.

Our approach is 'unitary' in the sense that we try in a detailed way to consider *every* problem as occurring in a social-animal-physical field. (PHG)

NO-THING-NESS

Jean-Paul Sartre entitled his major philosophical work *Being and Nothingness* . I want to show how Gestalt theory can act as a map, taking us from nothingness (i.e. the quantum field with its interconnectedness and fluidity) to the emergence first of identifiable structures and 'things,' then to self-identifications, and finally to the ways in which we stabilize selfhood, and experience ourselves as ongoing beings.

We start our exploration of Gestalt therapy and of the self with the undifferentiated field, the field of which we are a part, and in which (or through which or out of which) the world we perceive comes into being. In this field, there is process or movement. There are no 'things.' Some of the processes become relatively stable patterns for a while, and can be seen as things, entities and structures (if there is someone to see them). Furthermore, it is only in relation to these patterns that there is a meaning to the concept of 'time.' Time can only be measured in relation to regularities in the field: the seasons, the motion of the sun and the moon, a pendulum, a vibrating quartz crystal, the decay of atomic isotopes. Of course, without such stable patterns forming, there would also be no people to do the measuring.

But the field *does* differentiate. An example of the emergence of observable structure out of process is given by Coveney & Highfield (1991), writing about the patterns formed by heating oil beyond the point where convection arises:

"Heating a thin layer of liquid wedged between two glass plates can cause organization to appear in the form of a honeycomb pattern consisting of hexagonal cells of convecting liquid . . .The distance over which this hexagonal pattern forms is 100 million times greater than the distance between individual molecules." (pp. 185/6)

Here it is impossible to say that the pattern is a property of the oil, or the glass, or the heating. It is a property emerging from the whole field context. A change in any of these would affect the pattern.

Where the differentiation occurs (here at the boundary of the hexagons), there is what Gestalt terms a *contact boundary*. This is an interesting boundary. It is not separate from what is on each side of it (it is not, for example, like a wall separating two gardens), and it is not a 'thing.' It is, in fact, the processes occurring at this contact boundary that maintain the differentiation. The contact boundary both joins and separates, and yet is part of the same field as whatever is on either side of it.

We could also look at the formation of stars and planets out of a cooling cloud of gases. Once again, we are looking at an organization of molecules over a vast distance into identifiable areas with clear contact boundaries at ever smaller scales: planets, rocks, trees, plants, ants. Yet they remain interconnected: without the atmosphere of the earth, and the raw materials for nests and food, there would not be ants. Again the processes at the contact boundary maintain the differentiation, but the contact boundary is maintained by the whole ecology of the field.

Gestalt field theory begins with the *whole*. It is not that there are 'things' which contact other 'things,' but that *"It is the contact that is the simplest and first reality."* Perls, Hefferline & Goodman (1994/1951) (hereafter called PHG). At the boundary of contact a living organism both maintains its separateness from its environment, and finds ways of nourishing itself and keeping itself alive in that environment. Most importantly for us, what defines a human being is not something 'inside,' but the contacts in the person/environment field. The uniqueness of such a field is that the human being is making *choices*, acting *creatively* in the field in order both to live and to grow. The process of 'creative adjustment' in the field creates/defines the person at the same time as the person defines the creative adjustment.

In looking at the world, we recognize the 'things,' but underlying the things are processes — events which reorganize the field. If I see a chair, it is because there is an interaction of light in our visible spectrum, the quantum event called the chair, the quantum event called my eyes, and the quantum event called my brain. At another level, it is a function of scale: if I was the size of a planet, I would be unlikely to see a chair. At another level, it is a function of my culture: 17th century Japanese would not recognize a chair. At still another level, it is a function of human physiology: where I bend, where I'm comfortable. A chair wouldn't be a chair for a horse! PHG gives a marvelous process description of 'the present': "The present is the experience of the particular that one has become dissolving into several meaningful possibilities, and the reforming of these possibilities toward a single concrete new particular." This process approach says that the events out of which the world is built are what mathematicians would call 'vector quantities.' These are quantities like speed and distance, which have direction as well as size. In the same way, events are about being *and* becoming (as Buber would say).

Because of the centrality of field theory in this map, I want to say more on the subject, based on an article by Malcolm Parlett (1991). Parlett states five principles, which I shall state and then comment on.

1. The Principle of Organization

This states that "meaning derives from looking at the total situation, the totality of co-existing facts." (Parlett, 1991). Thus, in Gestalt field theory, there is no such thing as a purely 'intrapsychic' activity. What we think, feel and do — and who we are — is based on our interaction with our environment at that moment. This is a very basic aspect of the Gestalt approach I am presenting here. We do not just get a *sense* of ourselves from the contact boundary: the process at the boundary is actually the basis on which the experiences which we name 'this is me' and 'this is not me' rest.

We shall look more closely at the emergence of self from the field later on. Here I want to give an initial sense of selfhood as a second level of emergence from the field, based on interactions at the physical contact boundary (which is the first level of emergence).

2. The Principle of Contemporaneity

This is the Gestalt 'here-and-now.' This principle says that what is important in the field is always what is present, not what is past or future. We are not affected by the past, which no longer exists for us, nor by the future, which is to be chosen. What we call 'past' and 'future' are reifications (processes seen as things) of memories, verbalizations, expectations, fantasies: all of these being present events. We *are* affected by our memories of the past (and we choose which of our myriad memories we bring into the present and how we remember them) and our expectations and learnings based on our remembered experiences. We are also affected by our expectations, hopes, fears and plans which we term 'the future.' All of these are *present* parts of the field, as are all the environmental reminders of the past (people, photos and situations which in some ways parallel past events) and pointers to the future (diary appointments, lottery tickets, wedding dates, etc.). People in Gestalt therapy regularly change the pattern of the way they remember, the way they relate to their childhood learnings, and the way they move towards and take their parts in creating what will be. 'The past' and 'the future' have then changed for them. I shall say more about a Gestalt theory of time later.

3. The Principle of Singularity

"Each situation, and each person-situation field, is unique." (Parlett, 1991). As a Gestalt therapist, I should not have a rote response to clients. I am co-creating the therapy to fit in with the specifics of the moment: myself as therapist with this client, in this client's present life situation. Furthermore, in the therapeutic relationship, therapist and client are continuously co-creating themselves and each other. All generalizations are provisional, and subject to change where the field warrants it. It is important to notice that this principle is a long way away from any theory defining psychotherapy as recovering an 'inner child,' presumed to be waiting, innocent and unaffected, to be uncovered. 'Who I am' is an unfolding process, never to return to what was.

4. The Principle of Changing Process

This is a corollary of the last principle, and says that the field is continuously changing. Thus, for Gestalt therapy, homoeostasis and creativity go hand-in-hand. I need to come to some kind of balance with my environment (homoeostasis), but this cannot be a conservative act of returning to the previous balance, since the field is changing, and what worked before will often not work now. I must then invent new ways of balancing my needs and interests with environmental possibilities (creativity). At the same time, my environment will be responding creatively to my actions, so that homoeostasis, often seen as a conservative force, is actually seen here as the driving force behind creativity, and creativity makes homoeostasis possible in a changing world.

5. *The Principle of Possible Relevance*

This states that any part of the field is possibly relevant to the situation in which I am interested, and might need to be addressed. This is what Perls talked about in naming Gestalt the "therapy of the obvious." I remember one group, where an interesting process started with my observation that group members used an amazing amount of toilet paper. It is not just that toilet usage was significant for the group, but that my interest, and the extra awareness of the processes round toilet usage, affected the boundary, and allowed for new possibilities. These could include new patterns of toilet paper usage in group members' homes, group members' changed memories of me, a greater range of what can be spoken about in the group, or people bringing their own toilet paper!

FIELD THEORY AND THE SELF

How does this field approach carries over into the Gestalt theory of the self? Part of the problem in psychotherapy and in this book is that any culture has unspoken but quite definite ideas of what is meant when we talk about 'self.' Kohut (1977) said that the concept of the self is 'experience-near.' On the other hand, it is instructive to note that different cultures have quite different, but equally 'self-evident' understandings, ranging from individualistic Western views to Eastern views which emphasize the 'self' as a facet of the whole. These differences then underlie the arts, language, religion, relationships, politics and all other facets of the lives of those who participate in that culture. It also makes mutual understanding between different cultures very difficult. People from one culture can see people from a different culture as slightly or completely mad, and it has been known for people to be locked away for behavior that is quite sane in their own cultural terms.

There is a similar problem between practitioners of different psychotherapy schools. There is a growing interest in what is called 'integrative psychotherapy,' encouraging crossover between different approaches. However, there is the potential for much confusion as well as enlightenment, because different psychotherapies use the same words — therapeutic relationship, contract, cure, self — in very different ways. If that difference is not taken into account, we can come to a situation where the cutting edge of a particular approach gets blunted rather than sharpened by pseudo-integration with another therapeutic approach which is in fact designed to do a different thing. Of course, if the differences are respected, there is a potential to create very exciting new therapeutic forms: Gestalt therapy is one of these creations, emerging from an integration of psychoanalysis, Gestalt Psychology, existentialism, Zen, holism, field theory, etc. But of course what emerged has its own character, which will quite probably not be acceptable to adherents to any of the contributing approaches. And so it is with the theory of self that I am present- ing: it has its roots in many different philosophies, but it also has a character all of its own. At root, any theory of psychotherapy or philosophy emerges from a conceptualization of the experience of its founders. The Gestalt way of viewing the self accorded well with the experience of its founders (Fritz and Laura Perls, the philosopher and social commentator/activist Paul Goodman, and a circle they assembled round them in New York), and also accords well with my experience. It is complex to write about, however, and the reader would do well to take some time to check with her/his own experience: does this approach fit with and help to make sense of your personal experience?

SELF AND OTHER

"Now the 'self' cannot be understood other than through the field, just like day cannot be understood other than by contrast with night . . . the 'self is to be found in the contrast with the otherness. There is a boundary between

the self and the other, and this boundary is the essence of psychology." Perls (1978/1957)

What does the concept of 'self' mean in the holistic field? For Gestalt therapy, it means very little in itself, rather it is a *polar* quality with 'other,' just like 'big' and 'small' are only meaningful contextually, and in relation to each other. Underlying this polarization are two **processes,** *identification* and *alienation*, which are called the 'ego functions' of self. I identify with some aspects of the field and label that as 'self'; other aspects I alienate, and call that 'other.' But the form of the self is inextricably linked with the form of the other, and vice versa. The way I experience and configure my self depends on how I configure what is not-self or other (again, and vice versa). It is important to notice here that when I write of 'configuring,' I am not primarily meaning verbal concepts: rather I am pointing at the configuration inherent in my actions. For example, in writing this, I configure myself as teacher/someone with something to say/writer . . ., and configure the environment in terms of readers, people with interest (or no interest) in what I'm saying. Before this, I've been having lunch with my family at my wife's work, and configuring myself as family man, man having lunch, etc., and my environment in terms of family, food . . .

An image I find helpful in visualizing this approach is the drawing by Escher of two hands, each hand drawing the other.

It is also important to clear up one point at this stage. You may notice a circularity in my discussion of self: who is this 'I' or 'my' who is doing the discussing or the contacting? Like the fallacy in Descartes' "I think, therefore I am," assuming the meaningfulness of 'I' (in "I think") to prove the 'I,' I could be seen to be assuming what I am then defining. However, what I am stating here is in a way quite the opposite to Descartes: that the 'I' is *not* an objective fact, but a field event. It is the contacting at the boundary that is primary, not an 'I' making contact. The circularity is the same as the circularity of the hexagons in the heated liquid:

the process creates the boundary, which creates the hexagons, which can then be studied as things in their own right, in relation to other hexagons, the glass plates, etc.

What this is all saying is that my existence is not an isolated event. 'I' is only meaningful in relation to 'not-I.' At a simple level, I am alive by means of my relationship with the air I breathe, the sun that gives me light, the food I eat, the ground I walk on, the parents who gave me birth . . . As I say, this is the simple level. The complex level is: 'I' and 'not-I' am/is emergent from and sustained by the action of the **contact-boundary** between the Peter-organism and its environment. 'Self ' is not the same as 'organism,' nor 'other' the same as 'environment,' in this theory. The physical organism/environment boundary is the first reality, a base complex enough to allow the new level of organization of life, selfhood, and consciousness to emerge.

Philosophically, we are in the realm of the Eastern philosophies, particularly Taoism and Zen. The most beautiful, and also most philosophically coherent, of the works from this world-view is *Tao Te Ching* (Lao Tse, 1972). I shall be quoting from this as it illuminates what I am saying about Gestalt. Here I shall quote from Chapter 2 (my italics):

> "When people see some things as beautiful,
> other things become ugly.
> When people see some things as good,
> other things become bad.
>
> *Being and non-being create each other.*
> Difficult and easy support each other.
> Long and short define each other.
> High and low depend on each other.
> Before and after follow each other."

In this way, the Gestalt approach is not about expanding self-concept, nor about returning to an earlier self, but in facilitating the continuous development of self in relation to the therapist and the whole environment. PHG calls the self "the artist of life," and the development of self can be likened to the use of a wider palette of colors, and a wider range of canvasses to receive those colors: a more varied contact boundary. It is also useful in this analogy to emphasize that the artist does not need to use all the colors on the palette; if she continues to restrict the colors as her characteristic way of painting, that is fine. However, if the other colors are available, then the restriction is experienced as autonomously chosen, rather than forced on the artist by lack of choice. In the same way, self operates in characteristic ways (called in Gestalt the 'Personality function of self'): ways of contacting or avoiding contact, ways of being aware or restricting awareness, ways of doing things. This is fine, and the Gestalt question is: do I identify with this personality, and experience it as chosen; or do I alienate it and experience it as imposed on me? Do I keep my choicefulness, or give it up (a process that Gestalt theory calls 'loss of ego functions,' and equates with neurosis)?

So, for example, if I avoid anger, is it because I have freely chosen to do so, either because I want to avoid the consequences in this specific situation, or in accordance with my own chosen ethical position; or is it because I have alienated even the *possibility* of my anger from my understanding of the world in order to avoid the fear the possibility of anger arouses in me.

PROPERTIES OF THE HUMAN FIELD

What I have discussed above is a general statement of field theory. When we come to look at consciousness, selfhood and being alive, in other words to the *human* field, we are talking about processes arising in a very particular kind of field. This field operates at a very high level of complexity, and now I want to look at particular properties of such a field: predictability, unpredictability and complexity. Each of these properties links with corresponding human characteristics.

1. The field is, in a sense, predictable.
I know that my pen will not turn into a potted plant, disappear, change color. The person opposite me will not do the first two, but may change color a little.

Corresponding human characteristics:
Memory
Patterning
Homoeostasis

The implication for contact boundaries in the predictable universe is that there can be boundaries where there are observable, predictable and memorable events, patterns, or regularities. We could say it acts in a 'lawlike' way. So the train carriage in which I am writing this moves with me, while the countryside outside does not. It is a good basis for a contact-boundary that these regularities exist, but does not of itself provide the grounding for a self/other distinction. Isaac Newton described the universe as predictable with his mechanical theories. However, there is really no place for choice, consciousness, or selfhood in such a machine-universe.

The meaningfulness of "I" implies a predictably constant object universe to act in relation to, and with which to find an equilibrium (homoeostasis). My action now — writing — depends on the sustained existence of pen, paper and table, and at another level, the stimulation of my previous dialogue on the theme of "Self" with, among others, Hunter Beaumont and Sylvia Fleming Crocker. However regular the universe is, none of this regularity could produce a sense of myself as acting in the world (agency) without my corresponding attributes of memory and ability to perceive patterns and regularities in my perceptual and intellectual universe.

2. The field is also unpredictable.
The person opposite me is a three-year-old girl. I do not know if she will spill her drink over my writing, kick me, express the need to go to the toilet again, or scream. I do not know if the train will be on

time, be derailed, break down. (That the last is becoming as predictable as the first is not encouraging!)

Corresponding human characteristics:
Attraction towards novelty
Creativity

If all that we perceived was predictability, there would be no "I" because there would be no sense of "other." For the "I-experience" is of predictability *relative* to the less predictable other. For example, I can predict when my hand will move more than when someone else's hand will, or when it will rain. Martin Buber (in Kirschenbaum & Henderson, 1990) made the same point talking about dialogue (in his dialogue with Carl Rogers):

> Now for what I call dialogue, there is essentially necessary the moment of surprise . . . The dialogue is like a game of chess. The whole charm of chess is that I do not know and cannot know what my partner will do. I am surprised by what he does, and on this surprise the whole game is based.

The implication for contact boundaries of the unpredictable universe is that there will be some aspects of this universe that will seem more under my control or more predictable than others. So I will identify my selfhood with these aspects: *my* body is more predictable than the girl's body; my culture is more predictable than a foreign culture. Notice the reversal. Selfhood emerges from experience of organism (body) in environment; now self takes ownership of the organism (my body). In an unpredictable universe, creativity is not the opposite of, but necessary for, homoeostasis (balance): to seek to come to balance in an unpredictable and changing universe, I need to be creative, to embrace novelty, to be the 'artist of life' (PHG).

3. *It is complex.*

The interplay of the various levels in relation to me is so varied and interdependent that even the potentially predictable cannot be comprehended in its entirety. How loud must the three year old be, in relation to my ability to concentrate (and hence in relation to how much sleep I had last night) and my drive to get this written, in order for me to temporarily stop writing? Scientists express this complexity within systems in terms of *chaos theory* (Gleick 1987) and *complexity theory* (Waldrop 1993), and Prigogine's theory of *dissipative structures* (see Dossey (1982) and Coveney and Highfield (1991)). These theories explore the order that arises spontaneously in such 'non-linear' systems, rich in feedback and interrelationship, and kept far from equilibrium by the input of energy from outside the system, like the hexagons forming in the heated oil. These emergent orders show precisely the mix of predictability and unpredictability that I have described above. There are patterns, but never precise repeats of what came before. There is no 'linear' cause-and-effect, more a kind of mutual *negotiation*. As the field changes, the patterns are capable of sudden great change.

Corresponding human characteristics:
Awareness
Choice

With these characteristics, I can engage in the mutual interrelating that characterizes complex fields. It is useful to remember Buber's image of the chess game. The game grows out of our somewhat regulated, but unpredictable, responding to the environment's own regulated unpredictability.

I quote from Dossey:

"In other words, increasing complexity generates a need for increasing energy consumption from the environment, which in turn gives rise to increasing fragility. But ironically *it is this feature of the dissipative structure that is the key to its further evolution toward greater complexity.* For if the internal perturbation is great enough the system may undergo a sudden

25

> reorganization, a kind of shuffling, and 'escape to a higher order,' organizing in a more complex way.

> It is the quality of fragility, the capacity for being 'shaken up,' that paradoxically is the key to growth."(p.84. Italics in original.)

The contact boundary processes that we understand as life, consciousness and selfhood are founded on the complexity and fragility of that contact boundary.

With this non-linearity, the relationship across the contact boundary becomes interesting enough to make consciousness a pretty useful process! At the same time, complexity theory is based on the evidence that it is in just such non-linear systems that 'higher-order' properties (such as the self-organisation of the hexagons) would arise, and consciousness, life and intelligence are *par excellence* higher-order properties.

Without *predictability, unpredictability* and *complexity,* there is no sense in which "I" or "Self" are meaningful concepts. To each of these correspond identifiable human characteristics that correspond to them. And "I" can be seen as consisting of the interactions of these properties of the universe and the corresponding human capabilities. From a Gestalt perspective, it is not just that the universe gives form to my actions and therefore to "I" but that "I" emerges from the *relationship* between person and environment.

All this is not to say that self is unreal or illusory. It is created from the field, but, being created, self becomes a power to be reckoned with in its own right. In the same way, a baby, created from the interaction of a woman and a man, and emergent from the woman, has its own reality, and then reflexively affects the lives of its parents and others. The contact boundary between a human body and its environment is the interaction from which self emerges, yet I turn this round and claim the body as my own. We can see that, for better or for worse, the emergence of human selves on this planet has vastly affected the whole environment. This is what Goldstein meant by the term 'self-actualization': self becomes actual in its activity.

GESTALT THERAPY AND THE SELF

It is important to bear in mind that Perls and his co-workers were not talking about an abstract philosophy, but about a philosophical basis for psychotherapy. Fritz Perls was, after all, trained and working as a psychoanalyst. So what would this therapy based on holism, field theory and emergence of selfhood be like? First of all, Gestalt therapy is about *relationship*. We have seen that, from the Gestalt perspective, it is a mistake to look for 'self' as arising 'inside me,' and therefore to understand psychotherapy as 'inner work.' Rather it is a relationship process at a boundary of interaction between therapist and client. That boundary is not created by some 'self' and some 'other' coming together; rather, the boundary is prior to both 'self ' and 'other.' At the boundary, therapist and client co-create each other, and explore this co-creation. The difficulties clients are experiencing in their lives are seen as inherent in the ways in which they configure themselves in the world. In the therapy, the client can experiment with and explore new relational possibilities, while also taking seriously the impulses involved in *not* acting in this way (in a field approach, no polarity can be ignored).

There are some quite particular requirements for the contact boundary to be a useful birthplace for the statement "I am." At the time of writing, there are several terrible conflicts taking place in the world, which have as a major factor the habit of the former imperial powers of drawing fairly random lines on the map of Africa, Asia and the Balkans. These boundaries have never been able to carry out the function required of them. In some cases, other factors, such as a politician of great charisma or repressive power (or both) has managed to weld those inside the random boundary into a coherent state. When the charismatic leader dies, or the repressive regime is toppled, the state fragments. Either 'other' is inside the boundary — "I am not part of the same nation as them," or 'self' is outside the boundary — "Those across the border are also my kin." Interestingly, Jan Smuts, the South African statesman and philosopher of holism, made the analogy between the human Personality and the organization of societies and states.

> Just as in a well-organized society or state there is a central legislative and executive authority which is for certain purposes supreme over all individuals composing that society or state, and controls their activities in certain definite directions deemed necessary for the welfare of the state, so the human Personality is distinguished by an even more rigorous inner control and direction of the personal actions to certain defined or definable ends. This is the reason why Kant has called man a legislative being. (Smuts 1996/1925, p. 296)

Similarly, some ways of configuring the contact boundary between a person and her environment will be nourishing to growth, and some will have destructive consequences for the formation of selfhood, and for the person's contact possibilities. Gestalt therapy works with the relationship and the contact boundary to open up new possibilities for being and contacting. The therapist must be open to the growthful uncertainties of the relationship with the client, while avoiding invitations to fit into a familiar and ungrowthful pattern of relating. This can be personally challenging for the therapist as well as for the client. If I allow myself to enter the therapeutic relationship in this way, my contact boundary with the client can become highly energized, and new possibilities will open up as we are both moved 'beyond ourselves' into an existential encounter where almost anything can happen.

THE PARADOXICAL THEORY OF CHANGE

A central aspect of Gestalt therapy is that we do not encourage clients on a 'program' of becoming different. Rather, our assumption is that by accepting and exploring what is for the client, he can better 'identify with his forming self' (PHG), and thus will move on by the natural action of creative adjustment to the changing environment. As Miriam Polster said: "What is, is — and one thing follows another." Conversely, by having a behavioral end in view, I will discourage awareness of the client's objections to this and encourage the client to split off this aspect of herself. The continuing activities of this out-of-awareness aspect will then be experienced as 'symptoms' which are out of the client's control, rather than another important aspect of her functioning.

In the next chapter, I want to explore further the functions of the self in relation to the formation of figure and ground (gestalt formation).

Chapter 3

CREATIVE ADJUSTMENT
AND GESTALT FORMATION

    I have written about how the complex field has differentiated so that we can talk about 'events,' 'things,' 'organisms' and 'environments,' and, of course, 'people.' And emergent from this more physical level is another level of organization which we call 'life,' 'self ,' and 'consciousness.' At each level of complexity — field, organism/environment, and self/other — there are new modes of functioning. The field flows, the organism moves in its environment, and I live my life. Each higher level of complexity then has a feedback effect on the previous one. A dam alters the flow of a river, and a person's assessment of water needs might result in a dam being built. However, if we want to tap the change possibilities inherent in a field approach, it is to the field that we must always return.

    So, with this in mind, let us look at the functioning of self in the field. I shall describe the emergence of three interacting boundaries: the physical contact boundary, the self/other boundary (I and not-I), and the personality boundary (me and not-me). We can then address how Gestalt field theory approaches time and continuity of self-experience. I shall also speculate about how the insights of quantum physics might add to our understanding of the field.

EGO AND CHOICE

As I described in the last chapter, the differentiation of 'self' and 'other' is achieved by the boundary processes of *identification* and *alienation*. I now want to look at these processes in more detail. For 'the other' is a big universe! I need to focus on a specific other: what demands my attention (I have just felt cold air around me, discovered that the radiator was turned off and turned it on again); what interests me; what provides something I want or need (my hot coffee, in this instance). In other words, I am also using these functions of identification and alienation to bring close some part of my environment and filter out some other part. This is what is called in Gestalt Psychology 'figure-ground' formation, and is also what in Gestalt therapy is called 'awareness.' What I bring into awareness is the area of otherness on which I focus (the *figure*); what I keep out of awareness is the (back) *ground*. Thus, I configure myself as self in relation to that part of the field which I am now making figure, which in turn corresponds to my interests and needs, or the demands and invitations of the environment. Other words for this process in Gestalt therapy are 'contact,' 'creative adjustment,' 'aggression,' and 'response-ability.'

What all this says, in a precise technical way, is that the central act in human psychological functioning is *choosing*: choice of which aspect of otherness to relate to, and choice of how I configure myself and the other, and act in relation to that aspect. Notice that this process, however it's named, is not an 'internal' or 'mental' one, nor necessarily (or even usually) verbalized, but a process of orientation and action in the field, involving interaction, movement and encounter as well as sensation and emotion. For example, if my need is for food, part of my figure-formation will be going to the kitchen and seeing what is available to eat.

While we can separate sensation, movement and other aspects of figure formation, they are not inherently separate. Some situations are sufficiently complex, and our choices sufficiently crucial that we need to stop and think or verbalize before we act. This stopping and thinking reduces the liveliness of our contact with the environment, but in some cases (for example, in situations where I want to negotiate diplomatically with some powerful other) I am quite glad to avoid some of the potential liveliness! Or if I am practicing a new piece on the piano, I might need to work out what all the notes are before trying to play the piece through. The separation we then make is an interruption to the contact process (called 'egotism'), which we can healthily use in the service of making more effective contact in a complex situation. I shall say more about interrupting contact in a later chapter.

Notice once again the circularity involved in this process: I form figure and ground in relation to which 'I' forms. Again, this is not the circularity of faulty reasoning, but, as an analogy, the circularity of the internal combustion engine, where movement produces explosion which produces movement. A characteristic of both these circularities is that they 'come to life' and 'die.' Also, it is worth noticing how invisible the processes are when they work well: how the car and the self just 'purr' along. It is in difficult circumstances such as a cold climate that their complexities become visible.

Take a moment to notice how you are forming figure and ground at this moment. Experiment with moving your focus to different senses, different parts of your perceptual field. Notice that, as you make each new figure, the previous figure recedes.

ID: THE GROUND OF SELFHOOD

(A historical note: Perls and Goodman used the psychoanalytic terms 'id' and 'ego' as their way of linking with their roots in psychoanalysis. However, the terms are used in the relational

Gestalt context rather than the mechanistic and intrapsychic analytic approach.)

In talking about gestalt formation — the formation of figure and ground — I have left out a vital starting point. In order to develop an interest in some aspect of my environment, or an awareness of need, I must start with an unfocussed openness to the *given* of experience. I am passive, not yet ready to identify a need, want, or interest. Possible figures drift in and out of focus, any one of which could be attended to. I notice physical sensations more than when I am engaged with contacting my environment, and at some stage these physical sensations may encourage me towards a particular contact. If I am too quick to move into making a figure, it will either be some kind of stereotyped figure — what I habitually look out for — or whatever makes the most 'noise' in my environment.

PHG captures the feeling of this 'Id' or 'forecontact' aspect of self well:

> . . . the Id is the given background dissolving into its possibilities, including organic excitations and past unfinished situations becoming aware, and the environment vaguely perceived, and the inchoate feelings connecting organism and environment . . .
> The Id then appears as passive, scattered and irrational; its contents are hallucinatory and the body looms large.

This is very similar to what Eastern meditators call 'the void.' If, using Perls' eating imagery, the ego functions are biting off and chewing on the environment, Id is opening my mouth to the possibility of nourishment.

You may want to take some time out here to experience this Id process. Close your eyes for a moment, then open them without looking at anything in particular. Similarly, don't listen to or taste or touch anything in particular. If anything does become focus for a moment, let it drift out of focus again . . . after a time, let yourself stay with what becomes focus. You are now moving into using ego functions, or awareness. You may find you are perceiving things in different ways to your usual preconceptions.

MIDDLE MODE, AUTONOMY AND SPONTANEITY

There is a linguistic problem in conceptualizing the self in the way we have been doing. The English language has two modes in speaking about our actions: the active (doing) and the passive (done to). Yet what we are looking at is an equal cooperative effort between me and my environment, where there is no 'doer' and no 'done to' (or alternatively there is both). This is the '*middle mode*': neither active nor passive. A good example of middle mode action is surf-riding. I neither actively control my environment nor passively submit to it — trying to do either in the waves of the Pacific Ocean could be disastrous — but accommodate to it and ride it. The other name for this is *spontaneity*. If I am balanced and well-tuned to the waves, I will head in roughly the direction I want to go. (I want to confess here that this is not a skill I have.) PHG puts this quite beautifully:

> But the middle mode of spontaneity does not have
> the luxury of this freedom, nor the feeling of
> security that comes from knowing what and where
> one is and being able to engage or not; one is
> engaged and carried along, not in spite of oneself,
> but beyond oneself.

Spontaneity and autonomy are very different modes of being. Autonomy is an active mode, deliberate, chosen and free within the constraints of the environment. It is thus the province of *doing*: "I am doing this." In order to act autonomously, I need to commit myself to one important relationship with my environment (as, for example, I am doing now with my computer), and thus to limit my own contact possibilities to those required by this relationship (in this case, I fade out the sounds of my environment, which is a railway carriage, don't look out of the window much, put to one side thinking about the meeting I am going to and my family responsibilities in Manchester). This is the domain of ego: forming a figure of interest, and actualizing self in contacting that figure.[*]

Thus self is spontaneous and middle mode, swaying between the passive, receptive mode of id and the active, autonomous mode of ego. If I overbalance on the passive side, I remain unengaged, an observer of my life. If I overbalance on the active side, I lose perspective, and find myself on a treadmill.

THE 'AUTONOMOUS CRITERION' FOR GOOD CONTACT

The end result of the active deliberateness of autonomous action, if we are in good contact, is the spontaneous absorption in the contact. In my present situation, my typing skills, the feel of my fingers against the keyboard, the sounds and sights of the train, all become insignificant and I *am* the words I am typing. I can only do this if the demands of my environment or of my physiology are not too great: if I am reasonably comfortable, and my neighbor is not digging his elbow into my arm; and if my typing skills are sufficient to support the contact, so I don't have to pull myself out of the absorption to work out where the 'w' is on the keyboard. I will also be prevented from achieving this absorption if there is some 'unfinished business' pressing for attention (did I lock the front door before going out?).

If I can achieve this moment of full contact, then what is formed at the contact boundary is a *strong gestalt:* bright, graceful,

---

[*]PHG differentiate 'autonomy' and 'deliberateness,' which I am equating. It seems to me to make the discussion simpler if I do that, without losing any important nuances.

absorbing, unified and energetic, taking its energy from the whole field acting in unity. If something in the field (my neighbor's elbow), some lack of required skills (typing) or some unfinished business (did I lock the door?) continues to compete for my attention, then I cannot be fully absorbed. The gestalt will be *weak*: unfocussed, dim, energyless and divided. I will have to attend to the competing urgencies in order to be able to be fully present with my preferred figure and be able to spontaneously 'flow with the waves.'

It is difficult to overstate the shift in emphasis here. With this way of looking at contact, we can say that the properties of a strong gestalt are simply observable psychological ones, without compromising our relational approach. There is thus an *autonomous criterion* for good contact. It is autonomous in that it is not dependent on any theories of *what* kind of contact is 'good' or 'bad.' We do not have to have any concepts of 'normality' or 'pathology' in relation to what the person does. The questions we ask are rather "Is the person open to the givens of experience?" (Id function); and "Is the person acting choicefully to achieve this strong, bright, energetic gestalt?" (ego function). If the answer to either of these is 'no,' the question we pose is "What is being avoided/what is unfinished?." It is not even 'wrong' to do this avoidance. Sometimes I will need to accept that I cannot at this moment find out whether I locked the door, and bracket off my concern as much as I can.

Check with yourself on the gestalt qualities of your present contacting. Is it clear, lively and energetic? If not, what is missing? Have you been reading too long? Is there something else you want to be doing at this moment? Is there something in the environment that needs attention (e.g. opening a window to get fresh air)?

PERSONALITY: ON NOT REINVENTING THE WHEEL

There is still something missing in this account. The creativity and spontaneity of this way of being is very exciting and poetic. Yet, I also do other things. I make commitments over time: to my marriage, children and career; to writing this book; to acting in ways which are relatively consistent and familiar. What I lose in doing this is the exciting freshness of new experience in each moment; what I gain is autonomy, connectedness and intimacy, together with a reduction in the anxiety inherent in the unfamiliar. I participate not only in the unpredictability of the universe, but in its predictability. I can relate to this world because it has sufficient predictability that, for example, the computer I'm typing on will not turn into a flower, and its keyboard is roughly the same as that of the typewriter I learnt to type on (and I made the commitment to learn to type). In the same way, I can make friendships, commit myself to relationships and work and bring up children because I and others make ourselves sufficiently predictable that we can 'know' each other. In doing this, I can also 'know' myself, and it is in this sense that I am 'self-aware.' This is an important distinction, for, in the sense in which I am defining it, I cannot be aware of self directly, only at second hand via my relating to others, or by the memories and predictabilities of the life choices and commitments I make, or by taking on board how other people see me. *(It may be worth your while to check this out with your experience, since it seems counter-intuitive to say that we cannot be aware of self directly.)*

This knowable, relatively predictable, verbalisable (but not necessarily verbalised) aspect of self that can be called up in answer to the questions "Who are you?" or "What are you like?" or "How do you do things?" is called the *'Personality function'* of self. Personality has values, is autonomous and responsible, and makes commitments and relationships, limiting immediate choice in order to make a home for me in the world. It is not inherently fixed, and can be updated in line with the changing flows of my life. There are many moments that call for such an updating: adolescence, the start or end of a relationship, retirement, bereavement. Some people heed this call, while others stay with what they know, and try to face the new situation in the old way. Thus there is always a trade-off between the autonomy of personality and the spontaneity of recreating myself anew in each moment. At one end of the spectrum, there is the tired, obsessive repetition of Samuel Beckett's characters; at the other end is the butterfly, moving from one flower to another, gathering honey, maybe even mating, but not making any relationships.

I would like to make one further point about personality and verbalising. I believe that often the way we habitually describe ourselves is the reverse of how we are in practice! For example, those people who continually worry that they are greedy will often in their actions deny their wants and needs. That is why I stress 'verbalisability' rather than what we actually put into words.

People will generally have difficulties, and maybe come into therapy, when their Personality function, maybe kept unchanged over many years while the environment has changed, is no longer adequate to the situation the client now finds herself in. Either it excludes the choices needed to deal with a conflict or opportunity in the client's present life; or the client is avoiding the responsibility of autonomous commitment, and discovers that she is lonely or unfulfilled.

PERSONALITY AND EMPATHY

One of the differences between Gestalt therapy and some other approaches such as Person Centered Therapy and Self Psychology is in its emphasis on *difference:* the client is meeting someone who is for him/her 'other.' Rogers (1951) described the counselor's empathic function as

> . . . *to assume, in so far as he is able, the internal frame of reference of the client, to perceive the world as the client sees it, to perceive the client himself as he is seen by himself, to lay aside all perceptions from the external frame of reference while doing so, and to communicate something of this empathic understanding to the client.*

Notice how "the internal frame of reference of the client" and "the client himself as he is seen by himself " are about Personality. Given my understanding of why people come into therapy, due to destructive rigidities of Personality, I would question the wisdom of acting in a way which would behaviorally reinforce that Personality. Later, I shall expand on this, and contrast empathy with Buber's concept of 'inclusion.' For now, notice that the approach I am taking does not allow for the therapist to be an objective observer of the client's objective selfhood, since that selfhood is formed in relation to the therapist in the moment. The most the therapist can observe is the *rigidities* of selfhood, i.e. the Personality function.

What can you think of as major aspects of your Personality? How would you answer the question "What are you like?" How does it feel for you to imagine yourself as acting differently from these descriptions?

Personality serves us well when it grows in a context of Id (openness to the reality of 'what is') and Ego (so that Personality is a *choice* rather than a compulsion). People generally come into therapy, or find life overwhelming, when they lose Id functioning or make Ego functioning subservient to Personality, making only the figure I expect to make. I then live in a world I commit myself to 'seeing' rather than the world I currently live in, or I become a slave to the security of the familiar rather than risking creativity. Just as the contact boundary both separates and joins organism and environment, Personality both separates me from not-me and allows me to make relationships. But if I rely on Personality rather than Id and Ego, then it acts like a wall rather than an organic boundary. The person is under siege, and sooner or later the nourishment runs out.

THREE BOUNDARIES

I have now identified three interacting boundaries which between them define me in the world:

1. The physical contact boundary (it and not-it): organism and environment, inside or outside my skin. In Gestalt theory, we emphasize both that this boundary separates organism and environment, and that it joins them. Without my environment, I cannot exist, and meanwhile I am maintaining aspects of my environment, e.g. bacteria. I want to make the philosophical statement that 'id' can primarily be seen as a function of this physical contact boundary rather than 'mine.' This captures for me the sense of self arising from experience rather than self pre-existing experience.

2. *The self/other boundary or ego-boundary (I and not-I):* the operation of identification and alienation in the field of the organism. I begin here. The self can then turn back on the physical contact boundary and identify the organism as 'my body' and the environment as 'out there.' However, I can at various times identify something outside my skin as self, whether it be clothes or a tool I work with skillfully (in my aikido training, we are encouraged to make a stave or a sword an extension of ourselves). I can also alienate part of what is inside my skin as other (at an extreme removing a diseased organ). I might also have little sense of where 'other' starts physically, particularly if I have had little experience of physical contact in infancy, or if I hold parts of my body immobile, since reduced movement also reduces sensation. (My experience with clients who keep very still is that they are avoiding sensation.) If I habitually identify aspects of environment as self, or aspects of my physical organism as other, I will have difficulty acting gracefully in the world. I shall say more about such 'boundary disturbances' later.

A problem arises if these first two boundaries are confused, so that self is made polar to environment. These boundaries are actually quite different, as I hope my account of them shows.

3. *The personality boundary (me and not-me):* who I tell myself and others that I am and am not, my commitments and values, my character and sense of self, my home, my work and my family. It also includes what I accept of what others tell me about myself: how I am seen in my social context. More problematically, it will

include rigidifications produced out of fear of change or the unknown. *

CYCLE OF CONTACT

Looking at a single contact episode, we can put it in the form of a cycle. Hopefully, this will make it easier to see how all the processes I have written about work together to enable us to make contact in the world, and to be ourselves in the contact-making. I am using the words of PHG as much as possible, as they are very elegant here.

1. Forecontact: the stage of accepting the given without engaging. Figures are scattered, hallucinatory and disorganized, and can be understood as the sensing of the whole field, rather than 'mine.' The body looms large as proprioceptions (body sensations) flood the field. This is the Id function of self, which is here potential rather than actual.

2. Contacting:
(a) the excitement of appetite and environmental possibility become alternating figures as a contact boundary forms, the rest of the environment and bodily experience progressively becoming ground, there is an emotion. Already, ego functioning has begun, and motor response has already started: turning the head, focusing the eyes, possibly physically moving towards some environmental possibility.

(b) the excitement of appetite becomes ground, some environmental possibility is the figure, and becomes an 'object,'

---

*This is the boundary which the Polsters (1973) call the 'I-boundary.' However, they give this a much more central place, since they do not discuss or accept the relational view of self, and thus identify the self/other boundary in 2. above with the personality boundary (Philippson, 1996).

there is aggression in approaching and overcoming obstacles, choosing and rejecting possibilities, and deliberate orientation and manipulation. Self expands through the identifications and alienations of Ego: "I am doing this in relation to that object."

3. Final Contact: against a background of unconcernful environment and body, the lively goal is the figure and is in touch. All deliberateness is relaxed and there is a spontaneous unitary action of perception, motion and feeling. The awareness is at its brightest, in the figure of the You. Notice that Self is at its fullest here, while 'self-awareness' (focus on self-commenting, etc.) is at its lowest.

4. Post-Contact: There is a flowing organism/environment interaction that is not a figure/background (no new figure is being formed): the self diminishes in the movement from Ego back to Id. Personality is either affirmed or updated. As the figure disperses, there is an emotional tone which can be satisfaction and/or mourning.

Examples

Out of the myriad possibilities of awareness and contact (forecontact), I experience a dull feeling in my stomach and find my eyes moving towards the kitchen (contacting). I feel dissatisfied. As I move towards the kitchen, I look alternately at bread, cans of soup, cheese. My pleasurable response is strongest to the bread and the cheese and I make a sandwich. As I eat the sandwich (final contact), the bright figure is the look, taste, texture and smell of the sandwich coupled with the increasing comfort of my stomach and my feelings of pleasure. When I finish the sandwich (post-contact), I am aware of the residual taste of the cheese, which I savor, but progressively find myself becoming less interested by this. What next (forecontact)?

My son Robert comes in. I find my eyes moving towards him and feel warmth (contacting). Our eyes meet, and I smile and say 'Hello' (final contact). I feel pleasure, see his face, and hear his voice. Not having anything in particular we want from each other we then turn our attentions away from each other. What next (forecontact)?

TWO NOTES FOR CONFUSED GESTALTISTS

Those readers who are knowledgeable about Gestalt theory may have noticed that my account here differs from that of other Gestalt writers in two ways.

First of all, you may not recognize my definition of '**Id**.' The reason for this is that there is an ambiguity in the discussions of Id in PHG. Further, I believe there is connection between this ambiguity and the variety of different ways of understanding and practicing Gestalt therapy.

The definition I take from PHG of 'Id' is in the chapter 'Self, Id, Ego and Personality.' This is the 'zero point' of Friedlander (1918), pre-differentiation. It is a *selfless* time, open to the given, but without attachment to any figure. Fleeting figures form and dissolve, and "the body looms large" (PHG). I connect this position to my experience of Zazen meditation, and to the eastern idea of 'the void.' Let me call this 'Id1.' The other place where Id is spoken of in PHG is in the 4-stage model of contacting: "1. Forecontact: the body is the ground, the appetite or environmental stimulus is the figure. This is what is aware as the given or Id of the situation, dissolving into its possibilities." Now, if we take away the last bit "dissolving into its possibilities," which is rather pasted in from the previous definition, we have something very different, much nearer to what Isadore From and Joel Latner (1986) take as 'Id.' Call it 'Id2.' In fact, Id1 fits much better with Post-Contact on this cycle. Self diminishes, there is no figure/background. The problem then is in the ordering. A cycle has no beginning or end, but this one is put in a line from 1. to 4., thus making the void/Id1 an end-point, and a stimulus/appetite/Id2 the start point. This causes problems. **What Id1 allows for, and Id2 doesn't, is that the whole is prior to the parts, i.e. what I take as the basis for Gestalt field theory.** For some ego functioning/choice has already happened, and some separation of self and other made, before I can recognize 'appetites' or 'environmental stimulus.'

When either appetite or environmental stimulus become aware, this is ego functioning. The field is differentiating, a contact boundary is forming, the polar pair of 'self' and 'other' are emerging. One of many possible environmental stimuli and appetites are becoming figural. In Id1, there is not really a contact boundary. This is why the definition of Id1 emphasizes the "hallucinatory" quality of the sensing in this form. My eyes, ears and proprioceptors are, so to speak, proprioceptors of the *whole field*, rather than '*my* senses.'

I present a (hopefully) more consistent form of the cycle of contact in this chapter.

Secondly, you may be more familiar with another 'cycle of awareness' that originated with the Gestalt Institute of Cleveland (Zinker, 1977). It does not fit with the Gestalt theory I am presenting here, where mobilization and action are inherent parts of the awareness/contacting process, but it does fit with what happens with our awareness if we add delay, thinking and planning (what PHG call 'egotism') to our relating. Then the unified activity of sensation/aware-ness/mobilization of energy/action to final contact becomes split and sequential: this is the aim of egotism, to delay the action in a difficult environment, where we want to try things out in fantasy before living it out in the world.

Each of the stages of the cycle I present here involves a different level of sensing, awareness, energization, action and contacting. Each aspect is relational, as opposed to the Cleveland cycle, where much is intrapsychic. It is thus a superficially similar theory, but is actually quite different in its underlying assumptions and philosophy.

I will say more about this in Chapter 14.

IDENTITY AND TIME

A major part of what we understand as 'self' is our sense of continuous identity over time. So the Peter who is writing this feels connected to the Peter who was a child in London and the Peter who will be meeting a friend later today and going to a conference next month. As I have said, while a relational theory of self accounts easily for change, the challenge for such a theory is to account for this sense of continuity. This is what I will now address.

First of all, how does Gestalt therapy view time? The Gestalt understanding (Perls, 1969) is that, for us, there is no such 'thing' as 'the past' or 'the future' — only *here-and-now*. This statement has often been taken to mean that we act as if our history or future is unimportant, and we must only be aware of what is in the therapy room with us. That is emphatically *not* what is meant. The here-and-now includes our memories, which may or may not be accurate representations of what has occurred (and are often at least partially inaccurate, as anyone who has taken witness statements can testify!), It also includes our hopes, plans, fears and expectations of what will happen, which again may or may not be accurate. Reinforcing these latter representations of 'the future' are memories of past sequences of expectations moving into experiences and then into memories. Behind these memories lies one of the major attributes of the universe in which we live: *predictability*. What we remember is pretty consistent with what is here-and-now, and with our memories of the consistency of here-and-now with our expectations (because we tend to remember events in a way which is consistent with our expectations).

Without our memories, and the predictability of the universe, we could not abstract from our experience a *gestalt* called time, and hence could not move beyond immediate sense data to abstract a *gestalt* called self. Thus Kant understood our sense of passing time as an *a priori* template that we project onto our sense data. A relational Gestalt perspective would be that this is partially true, and that there is also some way in which this accords with how the world is. Otherwise we would not gain meaning and clarity by using the template. However, if we notice two things, we can see that something even more complicated is happening here.

VECTOR AWARENESS

The first thing to notice is that all awareness is here and now. It cannot be anywhere else. If I remember a past event, that memory, and the choice of which memory and how I remember it, are here now. Furthermore, any event is much richer than my recollection of it, however accurate. My recollection will only be of that aspect which I personally observed, together with images that 'fill in the blanks' and make sense of the experience.* If I visualize a future event, I construct that visualization now out of my hopes, fears, expectations and commitments. What I visualize may come to pass, or it may not, just as what I remember may have happened as I remember it, or not. But the remembering and the visualizing are present events.

The second thing to notice is that, paradoxically, I cannot be aware just of the moment. I do not believe we can be aware of discrete events except as part of a moving, changing process. We are aware of difference, of change, of novelty, and it is only in relation to all these that we perceive the event. This is basic to Gestalt Psychology. Thus I hear the note B differently in music in the key of C and in the key of E (i.e. in the context of notes that precede and follow the B, or are played alongside it), and even then only in relation to a sonic background which allows me to hear the tone clearly. I see a lizard against the grass only when it moves.

---

*This is an example of the gestalt psychology principle of closure, that we will perceptually complete something that is incomplete.

I can only stay aware of something static if I move in relation to them, if only by moving or refocusing my eyes. *Novelty* is an essential aspect of awareness, and novelty inevitably involves time (this is now, but wasn't then). Organismic self-regulation, except at the simplest, most instinctive level, also involves a projection into the 'future' based on memories from the 'past': from my experience, carrying out this action is likely to achieve this end.

Thus we have a very curious paradox: what we are aware of is here-and-now, and yet is only available to awareness through the flow of time. The way I understand this is to think about what mathematicians call *vector* quantities. These are quantities which have both numerical measurement and direction. So, for example, speed is a vector quantity, since it is only specified fully by saying how fast something is going, and in what direction. What I wrote above about awareness and movement or novelty can be para-phrased as saying that our senses are geared towards awareness of vector quantities. Furthermore, the here-and-now moment is itself a vector quantity, only comprehensible in its motion from past to future. Thus my here-and-now experience of typing is framed by my previous thinking and typing training and my expectation of the response of the reader in the future.

What we human beings bring to the experience of time is our vector awareness, and also our ability to turn process into things. Thus we turn this vector flow of here-and-now moments itself into a thing: time. But, if we are talking about a relationship, this can only be half the story. For we also know that the environ-ment we perceive is usefully illuminated by our perception, and so must be such that time is a useful abstraction. There is a very powerful sense in which we know this is true. Saying that we have the property of turning processes into things is a statement which is in tune with the concept of 'collapse of the wave function' in quantum physics. This states that matter does not have solid form in isolation from a relationship with an observer. Rather it is in the form of a 'probability wave function.' When observed, this wave (process) 'collapses' into one of maybe a number of possible physical states. Quantum physics also says that time can do funny things. The 'here-and-now' can have implications for the past as well as the future. To quote Zohar (1991),

> Two events happening at different times influence each other in such a way that they appear to be happening at the same time. In fact, they manage to reach across time in some synchronized dance that defies all our common-sense-bound imagination.

Thus the concept of time emerges from *both* my perception and from the properties of the universe which I perceive, and, in particular, from the relationship between us.

Furthermore, we are also part of that universe of quantum probability. So in the process of me-in-the-universe, I become solidly myself as a contact boundary ('organismic-me' and 'environment') forms. My process then meets the environment process to form things and events, which are perceived by us as vector quantities, i.e. having a direction. Then the change and motion inherent in this flow of events is naturally abstracted into our notion of time.

From this here-and-now perspective, we can look at the factors that combine to give us a sense of identity over time.

Memories of my development towards who I am now. Thus, I can bring into what I am writing now my philosophy studies, my Gestalt training, my pondering on theory, my purchase of the computer I'm typing on, and the touch-typing course I took.

Other people's memories of me, which again are pretty consistent with my own memories: for example, my aunt who reminded me of the time when, as a child, I overate and was sick.

Inanimate witnesses to my continuity, such as photographs and words I have written in my handwriting. On seeing these words, I will remember writing some of them, others I will not remember writing. Other inanimate witnesses include music I have written, things I have bought or made, sights I have seen, and memorable meals I have eaten.

My plans: I am on a train, *aiming* to go to London. I have memories of other plans, other trips to London (usually arriving there!).

My participation in other people's plans: I know that the person I'm to meet will probably meet me in London, even though neither of us live there. Update: we almost did not meet due to the innate unpredictability of the universe, especially British Rail.

My participation in non-human processes: It is spring, and I can see the buds on the trees. From my memories of previous years, I can visualize the trees in leaf, and the leaves falling in autumn.

The summation of these experiences in a universe with a high level of predictability is a necessary, but not sufficient, condition of a continuous self-experience. To show that it is necessary, it is useful to look at people's experience when the predictability breaks down. I am thinking of the experience of refugees, of people made redundant or homeless, people who are suddenly bereaved or their children leave home, people who win a large sum of money in a lottery, and suchlike. People in these situations often experience a fracture in their sense of selfhood, and experience their life as starting afresh. To show that predictability is not sufficient, first of all, imagine a universe which is *entirely* predictable. There is now continuity over time, but what is lost is the *boundary of interaction* between any one part of the universe and any other. It would be a machine-universe, where there can be no sense of *agency* ("I am doing this rather than that"), no otherhood and therefore no selfhood. Thus another necessary condition for the universe to contain self-experience is *unpredictability*! To paraphrase a Zen koan (originally about permanence and impermanence):

The monk came to the master and said, "I have been sick for the last two days. Please tell me what subjects you have taught that I have missed." The master told him, "Yesterday I taught on the predictability of the universe, today I taught on the unpredictability of the universe." The monk protested, "How can the universe be both predictable and unpredictable?" The master explained, "Yesterday it was predictable, today it is unpredictable."

CREATIVE ADJUSTMENT AND GESTALT FORMATION

QUANTUM SELFING

Let us recap the simple (!) stuff before going on to something much more complicated! 'Self' can only arise in relation to, and simultaneously with its polar opposite: 'other.' The first reality is the contact boundary, which forms the shape of both organism and environment, connects them and divides them.

On the everyday material level, I can identify this contact boundary fairly precisely in space and time as the surface of my skin. This is only fairly precise, since I know that there are molecular and submolecular interchanges going on at the surface of my skin, with a blurring of what is outside and what is inside. Even more observably, air, sweat, excreta, skin scales, hairs and other bits of matter are moving continuously between inside and outside. But on this level, we sort of know what we mean by 'me' and 'not- me.'

However, there are some aspects of my functioning which are subject to very different considerations. When I examine the functioning of my brain, I am in the realm of electronic interactions on the submolecular level — and therefore in the realm of **quantum theory.** And the quantum world is very different from the commonsense world of things. (This is not to say that quantum theory describes only the world of the very small, but this is where its effects are most available for inspection.)

I am indebted to Dana Zohar for the ideas in her book *The Quantum Self* (Zohar, 1991). I cannot adequately do justice to the richness of her thinking here, and would encourage you to read her book. My interest here is in describing some of the types of interactions in the quantum world, looking at the similarities with some of the phenomena met with in the psychotherapeutic setting, and then to go on to wonder what a quantum-style contact boundary would be like!

In the material world, there are things which I can in a moment touch and feel and maybe move, and there are processes, which I can experience over time and space. In the quantum world, this distinction breaks down. An electron, for example, can act like a particle — a **thing** with mass and position, which can exert physical pressure on other things it hits — or like a wave — a **process** with direction and energy, which can show phenomena similar to those we are familiar with from standing on a beach watching the waves in the sea. Which aspect the electron shows, moreover, depends on the measuring apparatus we use. If we measure it as a particle, we get particle behavior; if we measure it as a wave, we get wave behavior. Even more, we cannot accurately measure it as both at the same time: Heisenberg's Uncertainty Principle states that the more accurately we measure one, the greater the inaccuracy in measuring the other. Gell-Mann (1994) (who by the way obviously does not like the approach of Zohar) gives what I believe to be a very suggestive interpretation of quantum theory in terms of branching *alternative histories* with different probabilities. As we measure one aspect of the electron (say position), we move down one branch, whose probability then becomes '1' (certainty). The measurement of momentum is on another branch, which is not accessible from the position-measuring branch. Zohar and Gell-Mann have written fascinating books, much of which is beyond this present work. At the moment, I want to point out some similarities with selfhood as demonstrated in Gestalt psychotherapy.

First of all, we must remember that brain processes exist in the realm described by quantum physics, the realm of the submolecular and the electron. Thus, in describing phenomena related to consciousness — in which brain activity is central — we would expect quantum effects. Quantum theory is not merely an analogy to consciousness.

Secondly, in defining the active ego functions of self in terms of choice, Gestalt therapy is also speaking of branching histories, where ego is precisely the movement from the cloud of possibilities of the id to the realization of a single possibility-branch.

Thirdly, Gestalt points to the duality between events and processes. My experience of working in Gestalt is that, by our methodology which emphasizes the process or field aspect, clients come to experience their lives as processes in which they have a major input. Furthermore, it is precisely the process of contact from which emerges the thing-like aspect of 'this is me and this is my world.' This 'particle/wave' duality is also very similar to the Gestalt juxtaposition, which I spoke about earlier, between (wave--like) *spontaneous* behavior, and (particle-like) *autonomous* behavior. Selfhood gets its flavor from the interplay of autonomy and spontaneity.

Finally, what quantum theory brings into the picture is the beautiful combination of a very accurately predictive theory, which also says that the universe is not a machine, where one 'cause' automatically creates one 'effect.' The universe has an infinity of choice points, where an interaction (for example, a measurement of particle or wave properties) moves us to a new branch where the same cause has different effects. Some outcomes have much greater likelihoods than others. At the same time, the physical universe we know about has such a high probability that we can regard it as predictable. So we have exactly what we want to have: predictability and choice.

Thus quantum theory describes a universe which fits well with our understanding of selfhood: one with areas of predictability and unpredictability; one with branching choice points; and one having a strong relationship to the quantum effects occurring in the brain.

We can now look at the initial therapeutic interview and the beginning of Gestalt therapy. How does this theory help us to work with clients?

Chapter 4

THE INITIAL INTERVIEW

A new client (let's call her Jan) is coming to meet me, and we will discuss whether she is to come into Gestalt therapy with me. What is important in the first meeting, as we find out about each other and contract to work together in a particular (Gestalt) way.

Who is Jan, and what does she want of me? From the Gestalt field/relational perspective I have been presenting, these are not separate questions from "Who am I, and what do I offer Jan?" Both of these can only be answered in our meeting, and the answers are co-created in our meeting.

All I *can* assume is that there is some area of Jan's life that is unsatisfactory enough that she wants help, and that she has not been able to resolve this dissatisfaction in relation to the everyday contacts of her life. Further, I would expect that the ways Jan *tries* to resolve it would be part of the maintenance of her dissatisfaction (or she would have resolved it rather than coming into therapy), and that what she will ask of me (verbally or non-verbally) will lead to the usual failure rather than to a resolution.* Thus, I know that the beginning of therapy will often contain a struggle of expectations between me and my new client. In fact, if I do not get a sense of this struggle, it could be that either the client is avoiding a meeting by compliance/confluence with me, or that I am avoiding some differentiation with the client.

Jan will also be likely to be making her new contact with me in ways which are familiar to her, bringing her hopes and fears of contact, and her own way of configuring herself, and of encouraging the other (me) to act towards her in a complementary way.

●

Let us look at the different aspects of self as they might appear in this initial meeting: an initial Gestalt diagnosis, as we can see it. The information for this diagnosis must come from me as well as from Jan, since the self I am 'diagnosing' is actualizing in the contact (or lack of it) between us.

ID

Jan is coming into a new situation, probably meeting me for the first time, being in my therapy room for the first time, making a relationship which she hopes is going to make an important difference to her life. She will need to orient herself in this unfamiliar place. How will she present herself? Who am I? To what extent can Jan trust me? What will I require of her, and what will I think of her?

My id process will be an openness to my experience of being with Jan. I do not yet know whether it is appropriate to offer

---

*Gestalt therapy does have another mode, as a kind of meditation or growth practice, which is practiced by those who enjoy the process of this therapy for itself rather than a means to an end. This is the mode often practiced by people training and/or working as psychotherapists or counselors. It is very rare that people can reach this mode without doing a considerable period of the other mode first.

her therapy. I need a space to look and give myself to the experience of being with Jan. What is my immediate response to her? To what extent do I trust her? What does she elicit in me?

The active answering of these questions is the domain of the ego functions, but the appropriate use of these ego functions is dependent on whether Jan or I allow ourselves a moment of uncommitted 'being here,' opening to the 'given' of the situation, both of what is available in our environment and of our own bodily experiences. In a way, this is similar to the moment of receiving the menu in a restaurant. If I don't allow myself space to scan the menu and also be aware of my body responses — am I hungry, what sort of food have I a taste for? — I will end up eating what I always eat, or choosing something I might not like, or what's on special offer. If I take the space, I can play with my bodily wants and the 'environmental possibilities' of the menu to make my choice of meal.

So, for Jan, does she allow herself this moment of forecontact, taking in without attaching; or does she either launch in straight away and metaphorically pull all her clothes off, or sit surrounded by her fantasy world without seeing me or the room, either way drowning out her needs and wants in the flood of her fears? I may also notice that Jan doesn't seem to be in the same room — or world — as me. If Jan denies herself this id process, I need to avoid bypassing this.

J: (Not looking at me, and speaking very fast) I was brought up in a violent family, and I keep on making relationships with men who don't treat me well . . .

P: I'd like to stop you for a moment. I'm aware that we've just met, that you don't know me, and that you aren't looking at me. I want to check with you that you are giving yourself a chance to check me out. I have no right to know anything about you — only what you tell me or show me. I am interested to hear what you choose to tell me.

J: (Taken aback, glances at me) Oh . . .

P: Hello . . . I understand that this might be scary for you. But it feels important to me, especially with what you have already told me about yourself and your relationships, that you check out moment to moment to what extent you are willing to trust me.

Allowing for this id process has implications for my stance in the initial interview. It is not my priority to get a family history. In fact, I believe that with some clients, starting by asking questions which I expect the client to answer will set the pattern for a relationship where I am the authority figure who can demand information. This is even (or especially) true if I ask for the information in an indirect way, via a written form. Zohar (1991) compares the situation in an initial psycho-therapeutic interview with the particle/wave duality of the electron in quantum physics. Depending on how we approach the electron, it will display either particle behavior (and we can measure its position accurately), or wave behavior (and we can measure its momentum accurately). However, it will not show both accurately, and the more accurate our measurement of one, the less accurate our measurement of the other. In the same way, if on first meeting with a potential client I make my priority the beginning of our relationship, I will find out less facts; if I make my priority the eliciting of information, I lose out on the relational possibilities of the first meeting, and also have no relational context to know what the facts *mean* to the client at this moment in time, nor what it means to the client to tell me them. In Gestalt therapy, meaning is a field event rather than an objective fact.

My clear priority from a Gestalt perspective is to the start of the relationship. There are some facts I do want to elicit, later on in the first session: Jan's present physical state (am I working with her long-standing depression, or a temporary post-viral state?); something of her psychological state (is she contemplating suicide, or hallucinating, or potentially violent towards me or others?); whether she is on any mind-altering drugs (prescribed or not prescribed); something of her social situation (does she have any support, family or friends in her life, is she presently at risk of violence in a relationship — and am I at risk from a jealous boyfriend, for example?). I ask about these in awareness of the relational implications of my asking, and only to the extent of my contact with Jan. Thus I might need more than one initial meeting before we agree to an ongoing relationship.

Also, what is Jan's perspective? Does she want the kind of therapy that I am offering? Is she willing to undertake the kind of exploration that I offer? Is she looking for a 'quick fix'? I need Jan to think about her wants in therapy before we decide:

J: My boyfriend told me that I should go into therapy. I don't know — it seems rather self-indulgent to me.

P: I would like you to go away and think about whether you want therapy for yourself — to indulge yourself in this way — and come back if you want to have therapy on your own account. Then I would be happy to work with you.

I want to expand on the theme of the client's social situation. I will always, with a new client, ask myself the question "Is the client's support system sufficient to do the work she needs to do? Will she go home to an empty flat after the session and lock herself away with her fears?" If I believe the client is too isolated to safely do the work, I will want to start by helping her to build up a sufficient support network, either by developing friendships at a sustainable level, or some local day center or community facilities. If the client is not willing to do this, I will not work with her.

These are all elements of the 'given' which I might make figural at some stage. The first element of gestalt formation, which Gestalt views as 'id process,' helps to ensure that the figure is true to its roots in our meeting, rather than a stock response of 'this is what a therapist asks a client.'

EGO

Out of the 'fertile void' of my initial moments with Jan, I find some aspects of my experience more interesting or demanding than others. I become aware of some aspect of our shared field which stands out for me: or rather the becoming aware and the standing out are the same process. Jan is also making her own figure. It is important to notice that the figures we make are likely to be quite different: we are different people; we are in different roles in this situation; and Jan is in a new physical setting, while I am very much at home in the therapy room. So some of what is figure for me is ground for Jan, and vice versa — and even aspects of our field that are figural for both of us are differently perceived, as they are figures in relation to different backgrounds. I will track, as best I can, this process of figure formation for both of us. The questions I will ask at this early stage are:

> What does Jan find interesting or important?
> What do I find interesting or important about Jan?
> What does Jan avoid focusing on?
> How does Jan perceive me?
> What does Jan expect of me?

In what areas does Jan act choicefully, and in what areas does she habitually stay 'in character'?

How do I feel drawn to act towards Jan? What might happen if I did act this way?

How do I feel? Do I feel warm, or cold, or frightened, or excited, or unmet, or overwhelmed?

I remind myself that all these are likely to be mostly a reflection of how Jan *presents* herself rather than a statement of Jan's 'being,' which could involve all of these possibilities. I hold back from a generalized 'liking' of clients, which to me covers the developing flow of my responsiveness with someone who will hopefully come to risk showing her more 'repulsive' and less 'attractive' aspects to me.

Are there any major ways in which we could stop before we begin?

Will Jan tell me too much, then feel so ashamed that she doesn't come back?

Is she looking for ways to find me disappointing, or abusive?

Is she going to rupture the relationship through violence?

Is she wanting a contract that I cannot or will not agree to: to cure her cancer; to 'fix' her husband; to stop her smoking; to make her happy?

Thus, to continue our dialogue:

J: When I look at you I feel scared.

P: (Experiencing a 'pull' from Jan for me to reassure her, and that this would avoid an important area of exploration) Is there any form to your fear? What might I do, or you do that is dangerous?

J: You might let me down, and then I'd have to go away.

P: (Aware that this is a potential problem for our relationship, and also wanting to explore this further) What might I do that you would experience me as letting you down?

J: You might not like me.

P: (It is important that we do not establish a therapy relationship on this basis) I think that if I related to you on the basis of liking, I would be demanding that you continue to act in a likeable way. It seems to me too conditional, and want to be open to you both when I find what you do attractive, and when I find what you do unattractive.

J: (Thoughtful) That sounds strange to me. I always try and get people to like me.

P: It sounds to me as if you'd expect me to abandon you otherwise. What I want to ask you is that, if you experience me letting you down in some way, you tell me rather than just leaving. Is that possible for you?

The information I would want to be presenting at this stage is that I want to make a relationship with Jan which does not require her to reveal herself more than she would choose, and does not depend on her acting in ways that please me. In particular, I will be willing to hear Jan's critical responses to me, and still stay open to the relationship. I come to the relationship with a strong presupposition that Jan is potentially much more than she will habitually show me. However, I also tell clients that I do not have a right to know anything about them, but only what they choose to tell me or show me.

PERSONALITY

Who does Jan think she is? What is her verbal self-description? What qualities does she identify as being 'me,' and what polar opposite qualities does she alienate as 'not-me'?

Is this personality identification an integrated framework of values for Jan to live her life by, or a defensive rigidification, whose virtue is only to ensure Jan's acceptance, safety, or even survival? To put this another way, is this personality one which is adopted to provide a connectedness to Jan's life, or is it essentially a manipulation of other people to feel good about her?

I do not ask these questions as a kind of check-list. Rather, they are a verbalization of my general interest in the beginnings of my relationship with a new client, in its possibilities and pitfalls. A good beginning can make the subsequent therapy quicker and clearer. A beginning where important aspects of our being together are not explored can lead to us working at cross-purposes and a loss of direction.

It is important to notice that part of our contracting will be issues round confidentiality, fees, frequency, other ground rules (e.g. around violence, notice of cancellation, contact between sessions). For example, I need to tell prospective clients that my involvement in training and speaking engagements might mean that there are weeks when I am absent. With some clients, we might need to discuss how to deal with these, for example by the client writing to me.

I find these initial sessions fascinating and fruitful. We are embarking on a joint enterprise whose end neither of us can know. Our relationship is 'sensitively dependent on initial conditions' and the direction we set out on will affect the whole course of our therapy together.

Chapter 5

THE INTERRUPTIONS TO CONTACT

With its emphasis on contact, Gestalt has to explore the polar opposite that arises at the same time: ways in which we avoid contacting our environment (or, to be more precise, ways in which we do not achieve a clear, bright figure which relates both to our own needs and interests, and to what the environment truly offers us). What I will do in this chapter is to name and describe a number of ways in which we can do this, and how this might affect our being in the world and the process of therapy.

There are many ways to talk about these 'interruptions to contact': different writers on Gestalt theory produce different lists, and explain them in different ways. My aim in this chapter is to connect the interruptions to the Gestalt theory of self. Those readers familiar with Gestalt theory will find some similarities and some differences in my approach to some others they may have read. I am emphasizing different points, and paying less attention to some other points, which are commonly emphasized.

It is important here to point out that to interrupt contact is not of itself pathological, nor is it a problem. It is natural, and part of our self-regulation, to be able to defend ourselves from contacts (even important contacts) which may be dangerous for us, or, whilst not dangerous, might be too frightening for us. We might merely not want to be making this particular contact at this time. The Polsters talk of the interruptions as 'self-regulations at the contact boundary.' Perls asks what is being resisted, and what is being assisted? Where problems arise, it is because these interruptions become intrinsic to our way of being in the world, unaware and static, rather than being based on the realities of the actual situation.

SPLITTING

I am going to begin this discussion of the ways we can interrupt contact by looking at a very fundamental way in which human beings can disrupt their relationship to their environment. If my environment is such that to experience it as a whole is too confusing or overwhelming for me to be able to deal with, and I do not have the power to act on the environment to simplify it or make it less invasive, I can split myself. Inherent in the concept of self as relational is the possibility that, in the interaction of a person with an environment, she can form more than one self, each one emergent from a different way of relating to the environment. For example, if a child is relating to a mother who alternately clings and then pushes away, sometimes the only way the child can deal with the swings is by the emergence of a self-process to deal with each extreme. Maybe the child in relation to the clinging mother will be compliant, 'confluent' (see below) and quiet, while feeling frustrated and smothered; while the child in relation to the abandoning mother will be angry and attention-seeking. And in order to maintain the splitting protection, the two aspects of that child will each avoid awareness of the other aspect. One will at any moment be 'me' (identified with), the other 'not-me' (alienated from). Some people split themselves to an extent that they never look from one part-self to the other: these people are variously seen as 'borderline,' 'narcissistic,' or 'schizoid'; others (more healthily) interact between the part-selves, as, for example, we shall see when looking at retroflection below.

It is important to realize that, from this perspective, the two selves (remember that these are processes and not things) can validly be seen as two different selves, even though they can also be seen as aspects of one self. Processes can work like that much more than things can. Remember, a contact boundary can form where the process at one side is qualitatively different from the other side. In this case, a contact forms between two split self processes. This splitting process does not need to stop at two: some people with 'Multiple Personality Disorder' split into many different selves, each avoiding awareness of the others. These can have different personalities and even different names.

In therapy, people often find themselves acting in ways which they don't identify with themselves. For example:

Jan: Something amazing happened over the week. My boyfriend wanted us to go on holiday to Tenerife again. I told him I didn't want to go there — it's too hot and crowded. We decided to go to a Greek island instead. All the time we were discussing this, I was thinking "This can't be me doing this! I don't stand my ground like that."

The biology underlying these split self-processes is well-documented in Rossi (1986) in his discussion of State Dependent Memory, Learning and Behavior (SDMLB). Modern research on memory shows that, rather than being a kind of tape recording, memory is changed every time it is accessed, and the change is strongly affected by the physical and psychological state of the person doing the remembering. So if I remember a frightening event in the presence of someone with whom I at that time feel safe and comfortable, the memory will often become less frightening. On the other hand, if I recall a pleasant memory of seeing a film in hostile company, and receive mockery for liking a film that no-one else likes, I will probably find my memory of that film less pleasurable in future. Most people have a number of 'State Dependent' systems, each of which involves accessing different memories, behaving differently, and understanding the world differently.

Another example is that I am bilingual in English and German (German being my first language, but English being the one I'm most fluent in). When I'm in Austria, and thinking in and speaking German, I think and act differently from when I'm in England and thinking and speaking in English. For most splits in most people, we are aware of the existence of other State Dependent systems. It is only when we actually divide the systems as a form of self (? selves)-protection that we burn the bridges between the systems. From this perspective, the different selves in Multiple Personality Disorder are different state dependent systems.

We can even spend our time making our contacts between split-off aspects of ourselves. We can do this obviously, by talking to ourselves, or less obviously, by imagining that other people see us in a certain way (whether bad or wonderful) which actually has more to do with how we are seeing ourselves. One of the major advantages of interacting across a split is that such interactions are entirely predictable. They avoid the anxiety of a real relationship with an autonomous other, where something new and unexpected (by both) is being allowed to emerge from the interaction. Often a client will express a fear of 'loss of control.' This always implies a split, often with one side of the split 'controlling' the other side, but with a deeper significance that the 'control' is in the predictable and stereotyped outcome of the process. Whatever might introduce novelty and change has been excluded. There is also a strong pull to control the way other people interact with the person.

I shall show below how the subtle or not-so-subtle splitting of our self-process underlies many of the other ways we interrupt contact.

CHARACTER

A lot of emphasis in child-rearing is put onto 'character-building' or 'having a strong character.' It seems strange to talk about character as an interruption to contact. Yet there are ways in which this is the case.

I can choose to configure my relationship to my environment in a limitless number of ways: and 'self' in Gestalt terms emerges from that choosing/relating (remember that the choice and the action are seen as a whole process, not two separate things). We can simplify this process for ourselves by limiting the range of possibilities for relating we allow ourselves. Ways of relating that are within this range we see as 'me'; others, and particularly the polar opposites, we see as 'not-me.'

One of the main ways we do this limiting is by 'ring-fencing' those ways of relating and configuring the world which resemble people we are profoundly influenced by (either by wanting to copy them or by wanting to avoid doing anything like them!). So inside the fence could be father's anger or mother's gentleness (or vice versa). We are now splitting, as I have described above. So at one moment I might identify fully with this replica of, say, my mother, and at another moment flip outside the fence and act in wholly opposite ways. But it is important to notice that the potentialities and behaviors inside the fence are not mother's or whoever's, but fully and validly mine. What has changed is not my possibilities for action, but the putting up of the fence. This can also be called a lack of *assimilation* of this 'lump' of behaviors. It is important to distinguish between a low fence, which each part-self can look across, and a high fence, whose function is to make a rigid separation. I shall discuss the operation of this fence more when looking at introjection and projection below.

Another way in which we limit and simplify our relating is by settling down to habitual responses. There is always a balance to be struck between treating every situation as a fresh one, with new possibilities at every moment; and having stock ways of dealing with common situations, which is both less tiring and also less exciting and pregnant with possibilities. Thus 'character' as I am discussing it here (following Perls) is the same as the 'neurotic Personality function' which we discussed earlier, which we do not allow ourselves to update in line with our present situation.

How this interrupts contact is this: if we limit our potential responses to our environment to our own characteristic stock of relational possibilities, we then tend to limit our contacts to those that are, if you like, the other end of these responses. If we habitually look for support rather than challenge, we will gravitate towards or create situations and people who support rather than challenge us. Further, by playing our end of the transaction, we encourage the environment to play its end. If in my relating I act on the assumption that the contact is about support, I will tend to induce those around me to act in supportive ways. This way of relating will of course break down if I am faced with a person who defines the contact in a different way, e.g. understanding challenge as the most important thing. In this case, I may react with anger or fear or confusion. These feelings will be demanding enough that I may interrupt the contact with the other person. But in general, I will avoid contact with this sort of person.

I do have two further ways of dealing with this situation of relating to someone who requests me to act out of character. I can redefine the situation for myself (and if possible also for the other person) so that I can act characteristically. I can define the behavior of the other person as 'wrong,' based on an *introjected* view of how the world is and should be. This allows me to act as a critic of the other's behavior rather than relating to the person directly. I would probably not even notice that in doing this I will have taken the other person's encouragement and switched myself to the challenging side of the ring-fence. There are few people so judgmental as the non-judgmental judging those with strongly expressed views!

The other thing I can do is to see the person in an acceptable way rather than a more accurate but non-acceptable one.

"Well of course he's only challenging me because he's frightened, poor man." From the other end of this, it is very difficult to maintain contact with a person who is determined not to see you except as someone other than who you at the time are.

In the following sections, we will look at both of these possibilities in more detail.

INTROJECTION

At each moment, we are taking in and giving out from our environment in a wide variety of different ways. On one level, we are taking in food, air, solar energy. On another level, we are taking in sense data: sound, light, physical contacts. At a third level, we are taking in information: concepts, books, cultural information, language. However, we do not take in passively. Left to ourselves, we reach out to that which interests or nourishes us, and we pull away from that which is uninteresting, disgusting, toxic, or which is just not our priority at the time. Even the smallest baby is well able to spit out or vomit up food which he finds unpalatable, and turn his head to what is most interesting. And in our reaching out, we also change our environment to fit with our needs, wants and interests. A Gestalt term for this is *aggression:* each organism aggresses on its environment to make it one in which we can live and be nourished in a variety of ways.

However, from childhood on, we are usually not left to ourselves. The world of the young child is a complex one, with many conflicts. There are the inevitable ways in which children are dependent on parents not just for food nourishment but also for helping them to understand and survive the world they have come into. There is very little choice for the child but to trust the parents in most things. If mum says "You may prefer the taste of chocolate to the taste of carrots, but the carrots are better for you," she's actually right! However, then she might say "You may want to cry because you've fallen over, but eating this chocolate is better for you." The child will usually take this on board as well. This identification with aspects of the other (parents, teachers, etc.) is called *introjection*. It is the lumps inside the fence that I wrote about earlier.

In his first book (Perls, 1947), Perls developed a way of describing the developmental stages of aggression in terms of the infant's development of teeth. He spoke of the young child's 'predental' phase of total introjection. Whatever is swallowed is swallowed whole rather than chewed. The child's physical (and psychological) teeth are not present. Later the teeth come: both the physical teeth to bite and chew the food, and the psychological 'teeth' of experience and wider perspective (for example, getting to know other families and teachers with different values and ways of relating to the child). The child uses her incisors to bite off a manageable chunk of food, and then, when the molars grow, the child is able to chew up the food into a pulp, which her digestive system can then process to extract the nourishment and expel the non-nourishing and the toxic. Thus what was environment can be remade into part of the child.

For Perls, a similar progression occurs psychologically. At first a baby does not have the perspective to be able to make their own meaning of the world beyond a basic distinction: of nice/to be swallowed/to go for, on the one hand; and nasty/to be spat out/to scream at and pull away from, on the other. For example, "Bath = stinging eyes = nasty = scream." or "Bath = slosh around = nice = gurgle." This is total introjection. Later, as the child's sophistication increases, s/he can say "yes" to some parts of an experience, and "no" to another part. For example, "Yes, I want a bath; no, I don't want a hairwash." This is partial introjection, which Perls associates with the growing of the incisors. The child can bite, but not chew well.

There is a two-way illusion here: children experience parents as saying "no" all the time, and parents experience young children saying "no" all the time. This is both accurate and inaccurate. The 'yes' is usually said by just allowing the action to go unchallenged (whether by the parent or by the child), leaving

70

just the 'no' to be said verbally. "Yes" is said verbally to a child who is asking a question verbally, whether that question is a replacement for a questioning action ("May I draw on this paper?") or a purely conceptual question ("Does 2 plus 2 equal 4?").

The final stage of *assimilation* rather than introjection is "I like a bath and know my hair needs washing sometimes. I don't like getting shampoo in my eyes because it stings, so I'll hold my head back and you make sure you don't splash the shampoo around." Now there is a complex feedback relationship going on, not only with the parent, but with the shampoo. The child is distinguishing two functions of the shampoo — to wash hair and to sting eyes — and is orienting himself so as to enable one of the functions and not the other. Perls associates this with the growth of the molars, and the development of the child's ability to chew as well as bite off chunks.

There will always be some introjects that remain introjects rather than being assimilated, because we rarely see them disagreed with (for example, cultural introjects), or because their truth or falsity is unimportant to me (I'll accept that Manchester United is a good football team on my son's say-so, as I'm not interested enough to put in the energy to find out for myself). None of this usually causes me problems — although my cultural assumptions could well cause problems for others from outside the culture.

However, the path from introjection to assimilation is not smooth in other, much more problematic ways. Any human being has the capacity to inhibit the disgust/spitting out reflex in a specific situation: where her survival or safety is threatened. This is a useful ability, allowing me to eat and drink something bad-tasting if the alternative is death (say, if there's nothing else to eat or drink). The capacity can also be used by someone else to use fear to make someone else (often a child) believe what they want them to believe. (An American Army saying in Vietnam was "If you have them by the balls, their hearts and minds will follow.") The child in this situation (or an adult in a repressive dictatorship) learns to avoid standing out as different. It is as if their teeth have been drawn.

Introjection is not, I must emphasize, a necessary consequence of repression. Some, both adults and children, either fight back or run away or kill themselves. Introjection is a choice (whether that choice is made in or out of awareness), once a child has reached an age to make other decisions. Of course, any decision that can be made in such a situation can have bad consequences.

Example

Often in a repressive family where there are two children, one will become the 'good child,' giving up independence in return for freedom from punishment; the other will become the 'bad child,' accepting punishment in return for the extra freedom available to the rebel. Each then looks at the life of the other and says "I don't want to live like that!" Each child, on becoming an adult, will have a tendency towards either confluence or isolation (see below) as their preferred method of relating in the world.

I want now to distinguish three aspects of introjection, which are in fact very different in their mode of operation. These are:

Verbal introjects: These are 'home truths,' often preceded by "You know what they say . . . ": "I want doesn't get," or "You can do anything if you really want to." In our very verbal culture, it is easy to emphasize this kind of introject. However, these sayings, introjected from parents or peer groups, are often divorced not only from our critical faculties, but also from our actions! They may then *take the place of* real compliance with parents' wishes and become literally 'lip service.' There is not necessarily any real splitting going on here, although the verbal introjects can accompany other more radical forms of introjection.

Cultural introjects: These are the norms of the society we live in. They include (in England) conventions like driving on the left, or learned habits like speaking English; the attitudes and characteristics which are generally shared either by the whole society, or by the part we live in, like a wariness of touch compared to someone from France, or a tendency to believe that there are no English national characteristics at all. While there is a splitting here, it is a splitting based on a continuing situation: living in England. If we act in a countercultural way, we can suffer inconvenience or worse, particularly if we decide to drive on the right! On the other hand, there are some situations that are more difficult to resolve precisely because our cultural introjects get in the way of adequate solutions. For example, in a culture like the English one that avoids direct critical statements, it is difficult to voice disagreement without the very voicing to become figural as the problem.

As Freud pointed out, there is often a conflict between our desires and what is acceptable or legal, and one way of dealing with this is to use the splitting associated with cultural introjects to suppress these unacceptable desires. Freud saw this as a necessary taming of the wild 'id' energies. Gestalt, however, contents itself with pointing out the situation, and providing a forum where clients can find their own resolution to the dilemma, with as full an awareness of the possibilities and the consequences — for themselves and others — as possible. Gestalt does not take the side of society as now constituted, nor of the individual as somebody unaffected by society. Rather, Gestalt performs its subtle balancing act, and sees a person and his environment as polar and mutually creating each other. This is an important point to note, since some approaches to Gestalt have emphasized the individual at the expense of the collectivity: on the view of Gestalt I am presenting in this book, neither can be understood without reference to the other, and both influences the other. Thus, even our consenting to some aspect of society is a choice, and affects the society we live in. Adjustment in Gestalt therapy is creative adjustment.

Introjected way-of-being: We can introject the way of being in the world of people who are powerful in our lives: parents, teachers, the acknowledged authorities in the circles we move in, gurus and priests. We can also introject family *relationships*, and act out within our minds and bodies family conflicts and splits.* This kind of introjection is often pictured in Gestalt as a taking of the other person into my boundary, with the implication that the therapeutic need is to expel them in a process similar to an exorcism of a possessing demon. From the perspective of this book, we can see things differently.

I am exercising my ego-functions of identification and alienation. By identifying with the way of being of some influential person in my life, I make foreground those relational possibilities which I perceive in that person. I simultaneously alienate other (polar) possibilities. This is precisely the 'character-building' process I described above. I am ring-fencing some of my possibilities as 'me' and others as 'not-me.' But of course, even though I might put the other person's face on the area inside the fence, the relational possibilities are mine. I can only act in ways in which I can act! Sometimes, as I have said above, I build the fence so high that it is impossible for me to see the other side. And if I don't see the other side, neither can I be aware of the fence!

If the therapy is about exorcizing the demon, it is very easy to facilitate the client simply to switch to the other pole on the other side of the fence (as we could see in the example of the judgmentally non-judgmental person above). The subject matter of Gestalt therapy is the *fence* (the boundary), which limits contact and choicefulness. The aim is to hold open the possibility of *reintegration*, so that I can appropriately and choicefully act sometimes like the previously-introjected figure, sometimes unlike. Then I can identify with all of me as appropriate to the present field.

Similarly, there is the polar opposite situation where I ring-fence behaviors of a person whose character I alienate, and will not act in any ways similar to that person. For example, if my father's anger frightened me, I might deny myself anger, and say "I

---

*Thank you to Petruska Clarkson for this insight.

don't want to be like him." Again, the limitation is not father's anger but the fence. I deny myself the possibility of relating angrily. Once I can integrate and dismantle the fence, I can still choose not to be angry, but from a position of autonomy: comparison with father doesn't come into the process. What is more, I am likely to find that inside that 'father' fence are valuable attributes of firmness, assertion and strength as well as unreasoning violence. Removal of such a fence allows me choice in accessing these attributes in ways acceptable to me.

Either way, I need to be able to acknowledge and value both sides of the fence, and then find ways of dialoguing across it. One well-known way of doing this, often connected with Gestalt, is the technique of the empty chair. In this technique, adapted by Perls from psychodrama, two or more aspects of a client are located on chairs or cushions. The client moves between the chairs, speaking from the perspective of each in turn, and creates a *dialogue* between these aspects. The aim is to facilitate *integration* of the different aspects through the dialogue, and to create an arena where the different state-dependent systems can coexist. (It should be obvious why this technique is unacceptable to, and will not be fully undertaken by, people who build high fences precisely to deny the existence of the other side *and* the fence.) I shall say more about the 'empty chair' when I discuss the Gestalt experiment in a later chapter.

I have meandered widely in talking about introjection. I hope it will help readers familiar with the Gestalt terminology to understand the perspective I am using here. To recapitulate, the primary concept that I have introduced is the *ring fence* which defines the introject, and the splitting that takes place at the fence. Working with introjection involves setting up a dialogue across the fence in some manner: using chairs or other experiments. The aim is to facilitate free movement across the fence, which is the same as removing the fence as a static boundary, which in turn is the healing of the split. The Gestalt therapist is not 'taking sides,' supporting one side of the split against the other, or aiming to destroy any aspect of the client (even if that aspect comes in the guise of an abusing parent), but allowing this healing — and this, paradoxically, is the death of *both* sides of the split, and the rebirth of someone new.

PROJECTION

This is the opposite process to introjection. In introjection, as we have seen, a boundary with a significant part of our environment — a culture, or a person or relationship — becomes a template for an internalized boundary across which we split ourselves. In projection, we have already split ourselves, often through the process of introjection. We then *externalize* the split, and divide the world into those aspects that accord with the qualities on one side of the split, and those that accord with the polar qualities on the other side. Depending on which side of the internal fence I am currently identifying with, I will be acute to the qualities of that side of the fence, and hyperacute to the opposite qualities, those I disown in myself, and which I will censoriously look out for in other people. Not only in people: the point I'm laboring somewhat is that these splits and polarities become the basis for all of our perception, and the (animate and inanimate) environment and our fantasies will all participate for us in the projected split.

Let me give an example, which I hope will make clear what I'm talking about. Say my family culture emphasizes loyalty and courage, and strongly disapproves of and punishes qualities like getting support from outsiders in disputes with the family ("washing dirty linen in public") or running away from odds that seem too great ("cowardice"). If I introject this, so that I identify with a split self that is loyal and courageous, I will value those attributes in others, and may also be on the lookout for those whom I can see as disloyal, or cowardly. I might disapprove of these latter people, or be angry with them.

Furthermore, I will look out for these disapproved-of qualities in my environment, and reproduce them in my dreams and fantasies. I may expect my possessions to let me down, and put a lot of effort into surrounding myself with objects that will continue to serve me 'loyally.' I may have recurring dreams of being let down, or involving someone running from something. It will be rare that I (as a reasonably contactful individual) will completely misread people and situations, but my capacity for expecting the worst — the expectation of being let down being the worst for me — will be a distorting lens in my dealings with the world. If my experience or neurology is such that I tend to cut myself off from contact with my environment by alienating myself from my senses, my possibilities for projection are that much greater, and more likely to be very different from the reality of the situation. The less I take in from the environment, the more I invent or make up to compensate. The extreme of this is psychosis.

This process is profoundly ambivalent: what I disown in myself and project onto the world may be pushed away in my environment (the scapegoat); and it will also be something to which I tie myself, because it is something of mine which I need, but have given away. Because of the negative valuation I give the capacity, I will often tie myself to its most destructive form. So, for example, I will find myself more in contact with people who habitually run away rather than with people who allow themselves the possibility of running away from overwhelming odds. Systemic and family therapists, psychoanalysts and others have charted the ways in which we actually encourage people to fit in with our projections. I have already discussed how powerfully manipulative it is to act towards someone as if they were going to act in a particular way.

More than any other interruptions to contact, projection is an unavoidable part of being in the world. The whole Gestalt description of figure/ground formation is a statement about projection. We project the spotlight of our wants, needs and interests onto our environment. Our very language is a projection of the way we parcel up aspects of our environment. I quote from a paper from *The Gestalt Journal* (Philippson 1990) on the negotiations involved in contact:

> This negotiation . . . usually involves both projection and introjection. I *project* my skeletal structure and my need to rest my legs at times onto my environment to create a chair; I project the range of my senses (sight and my visible spectrum, my skin sensitivity) and my need for shelter or beauty to create the tree for myself. At another level, the tree that I perceive will also be based on *introjects*: primarily for me the English language, which distinguishes trees from plants and animals and stones, but puts together under a single term the redwood and the apple tree. I can make initial contact with another human being without introjecting, but in order to satisfy any needs beyond the need for that initial contact itself, I need to introject aspects of that other person (and the other of me) so as to know what to ask for, what the likely answer will be, what the potential problems are, etc. (Italics in original)

So, to be clear, the problems associated with projection are not because projection is necessarily problematic, but because we sometimes let the projection drown out other perceptions and other ways of configuring our situation, and thus deny ourselves some forms of contact and awareness. More clearly than anywhere else we can see here the truth of the statement that what connects us to the world also divides us from it.

PROJECTION AND ID PROCESS

Recall that the id function of self is the period before the identifications and alienations of contacting (figure/ground making, or ego functioning) begin. It is a process of unattached openness, out of which crystallizes my interests, wants and needs, and the possibilities of the environment. If I do not allow myself this process, I can still make figures by using my ability for projection. Rather than starting with openness to experience, relaxation and relatively defocused eyes, I can be 'on the lookout': tense and alert for some category of experience round which I habitually organize my contact. So, in the situation I wrote of above, with projections based on loyalty and disloyalty, I might look out for possibilities of betrayal, or for people I can trust. My preparations for contact would be to focus my eyes and scan my environment for fit with my projections. Indeed, in my experience, a good indicator of someone who habitually makes figures by projection rather than by id process is often in the unchanging alertness of their eyes.

The contacts made in this way would be generally predictable and stereotyped. The avoidance of id process, whose purpose is to allow for the novelty of this unique situation, is based on the assumption (or projection) that the novelty will be dangerous or overwhelming.

PROJECTION, TRANSFERENCE, COUNTERTRANSFERENCE AND PROJECTIVE IDENTIFICATION

With the renewed interest of Gestaltists in our psychoanalytic roots, two of the concepts that we are rediscovering are transference and countertransference.

Transference is a major factor in psychoanalytic psychotherapy: and one that links with Gestalt therapy in that it is based on the here-and-now process of the client with the therapist. The psychoanalytic assumption is that clients will bring to therapy, and project onto the therapist, the attributes of important people from their early life, particularly parents. This will be facilitated by the neutrality of the therapist, so that ideally the client gets to know nothing about the therapist, makes no physical contact, and, in classical psychoanalysis, does not even see the therapist who sits behind the client.

At the same time, the therapist will find herself responding to the client in ways similar to this significant figure from the past:

this is countertransference. Sometimes the therapist will find herself experiencing emotions which are being suppressed by the client, a process called projective identification.

By paying attention to the client's transference and to his countertransference, the therapist can get an understanding of the client's early experience. This can then be incorporated into the analyst's interpretation, and help the client make sense of his internal world.

The question arises: how do these concepts apply in a Gestalt context, where there is an emphasis on the real person of the therapist, who does not attempt to remain neutral; where the aim between client and therapist is contact rather than transference or interpretation; where the emphasis is not primarily on early experience? Furthermore, is there any advantage to distinguishing transference or countertransference from projection or confluence, concepts which cover similar ground?

The distinction I want to make is that the projections involved in transference are pointers to my basic interpersonal stance in the world, how I orient myself with significant people in my life, and how I encourage people to act or inhibit themselves in relation to me.

I take as a starting point Hunter Beaumont's analysis of contact in terms of constellating the field in ways which are relatively comfortable for the person or people involved. From our prior experience, some ways of self/other contacting will be known and reasonably comfortable; other ways will be tinged with anxiety and sense of incompetence. Part of the skill of relating to other people is the ability to negotiate with someone to co-create a form of contact in which we can both feel relatively comfortable and can hope to achieve the results from that encounter which we wish. It is this skill of mutual attunement which I believe underlies the phenomenon of projective identification.

Often the importance of this process of mutual attunement is hidden by its ubiquity, but there are two circumstances where we can only understand what is going on by noticing a problem in this area. The first one is if someone does not have the skill, either because of some organic (brain) damage, or because he was brought up by carers who also did not know how to attune to the child. In this case, there is often a continuing family pattern of people who do not know how to negotiate to get their needs met, nor how to meet the needs of their children or others.

The second problem is if a person has been brought up in an environment where acceptance was easily withdrawn, or the consequences of acting independently were painful or dangerous. The result here can be that the aim of the negotiation is not the meeting of needs or wants, but simply the wish to survive by acting acceptably. Perls called this *manipulating the environment for support* and distinguished it from *self-support*. To self-support is to orient myself in the environment in such a way that I am supported: to breathe so that the air can support me; to hold myself so that gravity supports me; and more generally to be in good enough contact with myself and my environment that it supports me in my needs for food, relationship and recreation, while reciprocally allowing the environment to receive from me. If you like, this is contactful manipulation.

To 'manipulate the environment for support' is to have a particular set of ways of acting, unconnected with immediate conditions in the field, whose only function is to get some kind of minimal support from others. This could be by presenting myself as weak, so others take care of me; telling others how bad I am or threatening to harm myself, so they hold back from criticizing me; acting in a threatening way to others, so they give me what I want but do not come too close; or saying I will do whatever other people want, so they will want me.

Thus being supported is seen in Gestalt therapy as more of a response to our stance in the world — in contact with our needs, wants and interests and with those aspects of the environment which accord with these — than as merely something people do for us.

Looking at it this way, I can look at transference and countertransference as clues to the client's preferred contact and support styles rather than as direct clues to early experience. Of course, often these contact styles were learned early on, but not necessarily. Is the client acting from a sense of what she wants with me, or more from a sense of what I am wanting from her, which she experiences as a demand? Do I feel called on to act in a particular way with the client, and what happens if I do (or do not) act in this way? We could also describe these processes in terms of projection or confluence, but in a way central to my everyday being in the world.

Since the aim of Gestalt therapy is contact and awareness, a Gestalt therapist must have the ability to approach others (in particular clients) with a wide variety of contact styles, in contrast to the ability to be blank. These must incorporate styles which are comfortable and uncomfortable for clients. The client must feel sufficiently met in a comfortable encounter to be able to experience themselves as being confirmed (as Buber puts it). However, as Buber also puts it, they must be confirmed in their potential, and challenged by styles of relating which they do not immediately find comfortable. They can then experience the emergence of new ways of relating, which add to the flexibility of their being in the world.

Such an approach would involve an exploration of the basic stances the client takes. This would preclude any artificial attempts by the therapist to 'create trust' (e.g. the ritualized 'trust games' that have become cliches in some therapeutic circles), but would rather emphasize an exploration of how the client decides whom to trust and whom not to trust; whether the client is in sufficient contact with his environment to be able to make reasonably accurate decisions about his level of safety, or conversely whether the client operates from a fixed pattern of trusting everyone or no-one, or maybe responds to specific cues like gender of the other person, tone of voice, etc. It is such basic information, of vital importance in the kind of relationships that the client makes in the world, that becomes apparent in the transferential encounter between the therapist and client, and between therapy group members.

RETROFLECTION

One possibility for a person with split self-process is that the split-off parts relate to each other rather to the external environment. This is called 'retroflection.' There are two different flavors to this relating.

1. Doing to yourself what you want to do to your environment

I can, from one split part, make myself (in another split part) the recipient of an action which I both wish and fear to do in the world. For example, if I am punished by my father in childhood for showing anger, I might actualize one split-off self that believes that external show of anger is dangerous. The same process can be put the opposite way round, however: I will have *introjected* the angry punishing father image, while he would probably have *projected* his fearfulness onto me. So my fear of anger would be on one side of the ring fence I spoke of earlier, and my fear-denying anger is on the other side. In a situation which might occasion my anger, **if the fence is not too high,** I will experience both the anger and the fear. Thus, rather than showing my anger in the world with the person or situation which has angered me, the angry part-self will attack the frightened part-self, which may respond by trying to placate the angry one, or with sullenness, or by agreeing with the insulting assessment of the father introject.

Again, notice that this relating is only possible if the ring fence is low enough that the two parts can 'see' each other. Often other historical factors are being replayed in this intrapersonal interaction: father's fears of expressing his anger towards someone his own size; or the child's protective actions to divert father's anger towards him/herself rather than towards mother or towards someone who might get father put in prison. In general, members of families tend to put their ring fences in approximately the same places — although they might habitually dwell on different sides.

Sometimes this interaction can be fully or mainly non-verbal. Our bodies are built for retroflection! Many of our muscles have 'antagonistic' muscles paired with them, which move the arm or the leg etc. in opposite ways. We can mobilize muscles to advance and retreat at the same time, for example. The dialogue between the two part-selves can then take the form of activating both sets of muscles simultaneously. We then experience *tension*. This all takes a lot of energy, often leaving the person feeling quite drained. The importance of body tensions as a sign of psychological difficulties was first of all emphasized by Wilhelm Reich, who, significantly, was one of Fritz Perls' analysts. Reich talked about *body armouring*, which needed to be worked through in a specific sequence in *body work*.

Gestalt therapy offers body work as well, but it is important to note the different perspective. First of all, rather than talking about a unitary 'armor,' the two (or more) opposing impulses are the focus. These impulses both need to be owned by the client, and a verbal or non-verbal dialogue between them initiated. Perls criticized Reich's approach by pointing out that the concept of 'armor' encouraged disowning of the process, so the tensions would be in a sense attacked, leading to the possibilities of the defenses turning paranoid (as Reich himself ended up). Secondly, this kind of tension retroflection is not universal where people experience psychological difficulties: In the terms I have used above, it can only happen if the fence has been built low, and thus can even be seen as a sign of comparative mental health! We will see below what can happen if the fence is higher.

A Gestalt bodywork approach would include:

Verbal dialogues: Putting the two antagonistic systems on two chairs, giving them a voice and allowing them to dialogue with each other.

Movement dialogues: Moving first one way and then the other. Exaggerating one side and noticing the effect on the interaction. Reversing a movement and noticing the feelings associated with the reversal.

Externalization of the process: Arm-wrestling, hitting a cushion, kicking, remembering that the aim is to raise awareness of and integrate the feelings and processes rather than to 'get rid of' feelings. In Gestalt, nothing is to be 'got rid of': The process is of owning everything, rather than disowning.

I now want to go on to the more serious form of retroflection.

2. Doing to yourself what you need from the environment

The other name for this is *narcissistic retroflection*. Here, the environment is either unsafe, so that I dare not risk getting my needs met from outside myself beyond a minimum needed to stay alive; or impoverished, so that what I need is not available. I therefore provide it for myself by (from one side of a split) acting on myself (on the other side of the split). Physically, if food is not available, I start to digest myself. Psychologically, I can do something similar. Think of the myth of the beautiful boy Narcissus looking at himself in the water and believing that he is looking at someone else. He cannot move away from the water without his friend disappearing; neither can the water be disturbed by the slightest breath of wind without his image of perfection rippling away. Under what conditions in the rest of this youth's world will he stay with his reflection as his only friend?

Narcissism is defined (by DSM-IV) in terms of preoccupation with self, coupled with a lack of empathy for others, emotional coldness and grandiosity. This can be overt — the undiscovered genius (Kenneth Williams: 'I could have been a star'); or covert, with rage and sense of injustice hiding behind a superficial humility (like the very 'umble Uriah Heap). Perls (1948) identified narcissism with retroflection. He pointed to the customary usage as being 'self-love,' but said that this is to miss the point. The narcissist is not capable of love of self or others (but can often simulate love quite well).

There are many ways of describing the etiology of narcissism: among the best-known writers are Kernberg (1975), Masterson (1981) and Kohut (1977), all from various parts of the analytic tradition. However, we have in the Gestalt theory of the relational self a particularly good way of understanding narcissism. Self grows by contact: with the other, the novel, the exciting, the nourishing. But what if there is no authentic other to contact, to be excited by or to be nourished by? Say the child's parents are sick, or physically or psychologically unavailable to the child, or so unsafe that the child does not express his needs to the parents. The drive for self-actualization (in the Goldstein (1939) sense: Self is made actual by my action/contact, with no normative content of the kind which 'Humanistic Psychology' has added to the concept) will often be strong enough for the infant to project her desired ideal parent onto the unavailable parent. In order to support this projection, the infant must learn to deflect any sense data which might contradict this image: this will include most real emotional contact! So the infant develops a sense of self based on retroflection rather than contact.

In this form of retroflection, the fence must be high enough to enable the illusion of contact to continue. This is achieved by the projection of the idealized parent. The price is a more-or-less complete inability to differentiate self from the environment. The contact boundary with the environment is not maintained: rather, it is internalized. The drama occurs between myself and myself, but often with such conviction that my environment gets drawn into playing a supporting role.

An infant in contact with a real human more-or-less available person learns to deal with the disappointments of those times when the parent does not understand what the child wants or is just not prepared to play with the child in the middle of the night, or any of the ordinary mismatches that happen between real people; any such disappointment to a child in love with an ideal projected image potentially opens the floodgates to an awareness of his real abandonment rage and despair, accompanied by a sense of dissolution of the self. As this infant grows up, this defense will manifest in an inability to show real warmth, an inability to separate image from reality, and rapid alternation between grandiosity (a perfect person from a wonderful family) and rage and feelings of inadequacy (always caused by others!) if anyone truly 'gets through' emotionally. Looking acceptable will be important rather than acting morally; the narcissist is not trustworthy, since her commitment is to a fantasized ideal (and to maintaining the fantasy) rather than to a real person.

A Note About Object Relations Therapy

For those who are interested in object relations theory (you may like to skip this section), it is worth thinking here about Masterson's (1981) statement that it is not clear from that theory how people exhibiting narcissistic personality disorder, who have not emerged from symbiosis with mother, can nevertheless often act quite successfully in interpersonal contexts:

> It is a tenet of object relations theory that ego defense mechanisms and ego functions mature in parallel with the maturation of self- and object representations. A controversy has arisen over how to explain that the narcissistic personality disorder seems to violate this tenet in that a very primitive self-object representation is seen alongside a seemingly high capacity for ego functioning. (Masterson, 1981, p. 11)

One of the successes of Gestalt theory is that it offers a theoretical understanding of how this happens, with predictions about the resultant impairment of interpersonal functioning that fit well with observation. First of all, there is no assumed symbiosis; secondly, there is no developmental task that must be completed before the next stage can begin — we can compensate for difficulties at one developmental level by our actions at another. This is similar to the experimental and theoretical approach to infant development of Daniel Stern (1985), about whom I shall write more later. Thirdly, Gestalt theory predicts that people exhibiting narcissistic process will show a lack of openness to experience, coupled with the use of projection in order to decide what to make figural, and difficulty with novel and interpersonal situations.

Working with Narcissistic Retroflection

Working therapeutically with narcissistic retroflection is completely different from working with retroflected impulses, as I described above. There is not sufficient contact with environment or self for that kind of ambivalent behavior to occur. Narcissists are not good at ambivalence! This kind of retroflection is not associated with body tension: they are often very flexible, consistent with their tendency to flow into an 'acceptable' mold. In fact, many narcissists are obsessed with fitness and health and having a perfect body. They may also have a deluded sense of their own bodies, as their senses are inextricably entangled with their feelings and their attempts to create an illusory world. So narcissism is linked with anorexia, where someone believes they are overweight even as they starve themselves, sometimes to death. Bodywork leaves narcissism completely untouched, although narcissists will be drawn to bodywork therapies, and can (in my experience) often be found working as bodywork therapists. Dramatic techniques like two-chair work will not have any effect: the fence is too high. A major factor in working with narcissists is that they will not see the reality of the therapist for a long time. To do so would be to drop the illusory world he has maintained since infancy, and to face the despair and shame of reviewing the reality of their lives hitherto. Rather, the therapist will, if possible, be drawn into supporting the client's internal drama. The therapist needs to stay available and centered, not wanting anything from the client, offering but not pushing for contact, aware that the narcissistic client is not really seeing him, and that the client's actions, which have the potential to anger and frustrate the therapist, are aimed at neutralizing a figure that threatens to destroy his world. I follow Masterson (1981) in interpreting this back to the client. As the client slowly (often over years, with many attempts to ruin the relationship) opens up to contact with the therapist, she begins to put the contact boundary in a more appropriate place to interact with the external environment, and begins to allow the therapist to support him/her in feeling despair and shame.

Many commentators (see particularly Lasch (1979)) have remarked how common this form of narcissism is in our culture, and it is very important for psychotherapists to be able to differentiate between clients who are able to make contact, however neurotically, and clients who merely simulate contact. Unfortunately, it is also true that people seeking psychotherapy must also distinguish between therapists who can make contact and narcissistic therapists who merely simulate contact well.

CONFLUENCE AND ISOLATION

For the next two interruptions to contact that I will consider, we need to recall the two *ego-functions* by which relational self orientates in the organism/environment field: *identification* and *alienation*. The ability to alienate allows for a self/other boundary to be made in the first place; the ability to identify allows for interaction and contact across the boundary, so that the boundary simultaneously separates and joins. There are circumstances in which people fear and avoid one or other of these ego-functions, and we are going to look at these now.

There is a basic existential polarity which is being enacted here: the polarity of "I am in charge of my life; I am the measure of what is right." versus "I only exist as a small part of a larger context: The value and course of my life are primarily provided by this larger context." In *confluence*, I identify with the latter pole; in *isolation,* I identify with the former. I shall write below about the problems inherent in *habitual* confluence and/or isolation; it is worthwhile once again remembering that it is the habitual, unaware functioning (loss of ego function or choicefulness) that is the problem, not the polarities. It is also useful to go back to the discussion above on spontaneity and comparing this with confluence — "going with the flow"; and on autonomy and comparing this with isolation — "I am in charge."

CONFLUENCE

"You fill up my senses." (John Denver)

In confluence (which can be translated 'flowing together'), the ability that I put aside is that of alienation: either in relation to a particular aspect of the environment, or in relation to the environment as a whole. But something important happens when I do this habitually. I will have to ring-fence and alienate a whole area of will, decisiveness, autonomy and self-worth, all summed up by the concept of *aggression*. This latter term is used in the Gestalt sense as a vital need of an organism functioning in the world: it is the (literal and metaphorical) biting and chewing that we looked at when considering introjection.

I aggress on my environment in order to assimilate part of it to myself. This food becomes physically part of me, this knowledge becomes part of what I know, this ground is the ground on which I stand. In confluence, I do not allow myself this aggression, and project it onto my environment: a person or a job or a belief system to which I assimilate myself, which in effect aggressively swallows me (or down whose throat I push myself). At the same time, I retroflect my impulse to alienate, and alienate my own needs and interests. Putting this another way, if I do not allow myself alienation, I disrupt my process of making some aspects of my environment into (back)ground.

All this can happen at many different levels. I may be perfectly happy to accept all the conventions of my society or family, and not wish to distance myself sufficiently to question them. In other circumstances I will be able to know what I choose and what I do not. Neurotically though, I may chronically deny all possibilities of alienation. Neurotic confluence can thus be seen as being awash in a sea of undifferentiated figure, with insufficient contact with myself to be able to orient myself in relation to that sea.

I have written above about the way in which we tend to bind ourselves to that part of the environment onto which we have projected important aspects of ourselves, and encourage them to act in accordance with our projection. So, too, if I am in confluence with someone and projecting my aggression onto him/her, I will bind myself to that person, and work hard (even aggressively!) to encourage them to accept my mirroring of them. For example, it is a well-known trap for psychotherapists and trainers to pick up clients' wishes for them to be godlike and to act as if they had all the powers the clients think they have.

In discussing narcissistic retroflection above, we have come across one of the major components of confluence and isolation: The lack of a boundary of contact between self and other. More accurately, I do not connect the self/other boundary with the physical contact boundary of organism and environment, where I will be helped to orientate and grow. The aggressing self includes another person's wants, perspectives and rules; the 'other,' against which we express our aggression, is an aspect of ourselves. We have also noted that, in doing this, I can avoid relating to an otherness that can bring us new, and potentially frightening, possibilities.

I shall give some examples of different levels of confluence:

A couple, both in confluence with each other

Here both people in a relationship are acting as if there is only one entity between them: There is a 'we' but no 'I.' 'We' have likes and dislikes, 'we' know what each person will do or want in any particular situation. But being Gestalt and therefore relational, we need to look at both sides of this. A requirement for me to know what you want before you ask is that you give up your ability to surprise me, to act out of character, to act differently to my past experience of you. In order for this to happen, we need to avoid any external disturbance of our 'we-ness' from our environment. If we want to maintain our confluence, there is no such thing as a 'safe emergency': Safety is a product of a mutually-held and rigid boundary against anything emerging from our environment. Again, this is not one-way: The motivation for me to seek to merge with a predictable other is likely to include my wish to avoid what the Prayer Book beautifully calls 'the changes and chances of this fleeting world.' So I like to look at the process of confluence between two people as:

1) dissolved boundary between the people;
2) impermeable boundary between the couple and their environment;
3) each person in the couple splitting his or her self-process, with their spontaneity and unpredictability disowned as dangerous and destructive, and projected onto the environment.

While the confluence lasts, neither person would usually dream of going into therapy! They would only perceive problems arising if either one of the couple decided to develop a more independent life; or if the environment took a hand: A holiday affair, or the hospitalization or death of one partner. (It is frequently observed by doctors that, in a very confluent couple, when one dies, the other often dies soon afterwards.) Where the crisis is precipitated by one partner expanding her horizons, the couple will often seek couples therapy, where the strong implication will be that the problem lies with the partner who is moving away from the confluence. Both might be quite willing to believe this is so!

There is often a marked mismatch between such a couple who come to therapy, and a therapist who values individuality, and sees confluence as an undiluted evil. Interesting (but not very helpful) things can happen if the relationship-disturbing partner then shifts from developing spontaneity to confluence with the therapist's world-view. It is important that a Gestalt therapy affirms the value of the ego-function of identification ("I am the same"), and simultaneously offer the possibility of freely-chosen proportions of alienation ("I am different"), knowing that to choose this to any extent will be new and scary, and it will be easier for the alienation to be exercised by rejecting the therapist.

Sadomasochistic confluence

Here there is one person who says to another person or group of people, "I'm totally yours: do what you want with me." The role of the other person or group is that they accept the sacrifice and agree to, or demand, the other person's absolute obedience. Their version of confluence is that they also want there to be just one entity. The masochist and the sadist become equally bound to each other. This can be very blatant:

Miss Martindale, former headmistress of St. Bride's School for adult women seeking the chastisement meted out at traditional girls' schools, is publishing a Female Disciplinary Manual ' . . . Discipline is a fundamental human need to which many people are returning,' claims Miss Martindale (*Guardian 6.2.95*).

Traditionally, it was seen as the man's duty to command his wife, and the duty of both parents to command the children. In the church marriage service, the woman vowed to obey the man. Of course, what happened in the marriage could be quite different from what was vowed, and in many couples the woman had an equal say in the relationship, or even was the one who did the commanding. However, it left the way open to a man who could see his manhood as being verified each time he issued a command and was obeyed by his wife; and to a woman who, projecting her own aggression, could see her womanhood in handing over responsibility to a husband who would command her — and may be contemptuous of a man who did not.

Confluence with work or status

Confluent relationships do not just occur in marriages or non-married couples: They can happen in religious settings, work settings, clubs and professional associations as well. I know that one of the things I enjoyed about starting aikido was having a time each week when I handed over responsibility to someone else to teach me, where my function was to obey: It was a relief from my work, where I made decisions all the time. Unfortunately, seventeen years on, I now spend quite a lot of my time teaching aikido!

This kind of confluence can be very restful and healthy. However, as with the other interruptions to contact, it can become a way of life. I could define myself in terms of, and be confluent with, my work or my role in life — 'helper' or 'victim' or 'successful businessman' — and lose any sense of myself beyond this identification. I might even split into a number of different state-dependent identification systems, being the dominant father in the home, and an obedient functionary at work; or conversely being the strong decisive boss at work, and indecisive and waiting to be looked after or told what to do at home. What I give up in these systems is my ability to choose between a range of ways of being in any situation I find myself in.

Perls (1969) saw this 'synthetic,' 'as-if,' or 'role-playing' layer as one of the layers of a neurotic process. Once we have gone beyond the meaningless 'cliche' layer of formalized greeting, we avoid the anxiety of choice by playing a safe, known role. Perls (1978) talks about this layer more positively when he speaks about a different set of five layers: One much nearer to a developmental theory. I shall say more about this theory later: Here I shall just quote:

> But realize that whatever society is, and does, is an
> 'as if' function. It is a game, a game unfortunately,
> which many people take damn seriously . . . You can
> see that this 'as if' function is already less intense
> than the real function.

Some confluence with/adaptation to our partners, work or social setting and culture is necessary and desirable (as I have been saying in my discussion of transference). Gestalt offers the prospect of being aware of the way I am adapting, so that I can decide when and how much to adapt, and can realize when I have denied myself the possibilities of differentiation which I would need to deal with a particular difficulty in my present life.

ISOLATION

"We're two of a kind, silence and I.
We need a chance to talk things over." (Alan Parsons)

When I habitually isolate myself, I put aside my possibility for *identification* with other people, rather projecting this onto my environment, which I then experience as wanting to engulf me. I will be ring fencing my contact functions (my five senses, and my ability to communicate), and retroflecting my impulse for contact so that I make a more predictable and controllable contact with a split-off aspect of myself. I also put aside my id function of openness to the potential of my situation. Thus I deny my ability to make a figure by identifying with aspects of my environment.

Even though there will be images of engulfment, the truth of the matter will often be that what I remember and fear in contact is abandonment. Between my projected images of engulfment and my fears of abandonment, I will experience any close relating as outside my possibilities. Again I am awash, but now in a sea of my own projections. I could also retroflect my energy for aggressive or spontaneous contact in the world into rumination and fantasy. Ironically, since the projections are colored by my fears, the content of these fantasy contacts will often be far more hurtful than the actual environment would ever be. By acting in fantasy, I experience myself as more able to orient myself, but not in relation to my actual environment. From outside, I am seen to be acting strangely, self-centredly and probably ineffectively. In a therapy group, I am thinking of people who sit with their eyes either defocused, or focused on the carpet. At the same time, they would very often believe that they are seeing the group. However, the group they see is mainly their projection.

Once again, underlying this is the process of narcissistic retroflection. In the absence of a relationship with my environ-

ment, I will instead make my relationship with my nar-
cissus-reflection: Another aspect of myself. I will give this
'pseudo-environment' the flavor either of my fears about the world,
in which case I will act in a manner which we could call paranoid;
or in the flavor of my idealized wants from the world and from
other people, in which case I will attach myself to people whom I
will perceive as supremely worthwhile, and as wanting to treat me
as supremely special.

An image which I find useful and descriptive is that of a
hollow metal sphere with a polished reflective interior. A person
sitting in the interior of this sphere will not be in contact with the
world outside it, but will be able to convince himself that what he
sees all around is the external world rather than a reflection of
himself. This image is, of course, an oversimplification. Few people
isolate themselves so radically; most will have some sense of the
real external world, although their strong tendency will be to focus
on their projections rather than the reality, especially in situations
where they have an emotional reaction. However, to see the extent
to which the image can take over from the reality, we only need to
think of the process of people 'with' anorexia nervosa, who will
usually be showing this narcissistic process. They will be able to
convince themselves that they are fine and happy, even while they
are starving to death.

It is inherent in the field approach in Gestalt therapy that,
if the environment is habitually avoided, the very act of this avoidance is destructive and limiting of the self; and conversely in
habitual confluence, the avoidance of self is limiting of the
environment. However, the non-habitual forms of confluence and
isolation, described in Gestalt therapy as spontaneity and autonomy, are vital aspects of our relating of, and indeed configuration
of, ourselves and our environment.

EGOTISM

Consider two different situations. I am drinking a glass of
wine while writing this. The glass is beside me, and the residual

taste of the powerful Shiraz grape is in my mouth. Every now and again, I see the glass, and reach towards it to take another sip. I do not verbalized the process, nor divide it into a cognitive stage and an action stage. The relationship between me and the wine is direct. The other situation was when I was at a business meeting. I had a number of different ways I could contact people here, and it was not a straightforward matter to decide which way I would choose. My initial response was to move into 'internal' activity, a mixture of fantasy and subvocal verbalization. What did I want to offer and to get here, how would people respond, what were the risks? I, in effect, created a symbolic counterpart of the environment I was relating to, and consulted this before choosing how to act in relation to my real environment. Thus, I said some things, and did not say other things, showed some of my feelings and did not show other feelings.

It is important to be aware that, in the second case, I at times interrupted my contact with the complex environment in order to be able to choose the kind of contact I would make. I, and also the other people present, acted in this way in order to achieve a result much more complicated than to renew the taste of wine in my mouth, a result that would continue to emerge in the period following our meeting, and which already involves at least two further projected meetings. It is also useful to note that, if I did this all the time at the meeting, I would not be acting to make contact, but rather to manipulate the meeting to act in the way I wanted, while not allowing for the possibility of being myself affected by others.

Finally, it is important to notice that, in creating a synthetic replica environment, I am also creating a synthetic replica self to relate to this environment, which I can watch in its activity and evaluate whether I want to risk going that route in the real environment. This is what is usually called *self-awareness*, and it is only of such a replica that I can actually be aware, since the act of 'self-awareness' breaks the contact on which the self is based. We have already met the accumulation of such 'self-awarenesses' in our discussion of the personality function of self.

This deliberate delaying of contact into subvocal verbalization and fantasy is called *egotism*. In its non-pathological form, it is an interruption to or slowing down of immediate contact to allow for a more useful contact when I am ready to re-engage. As such, it is an important component of autonomous functioning, with a trade-off in loss of spontaneity. However, if I live my life in chronically complex relationship to my environment, either because my environment is always complex, or because I bring to that environment enough 'unfinished business' that I complicate all my relating (for example, looking out for threats, choosing difficult situations over easy ones), then several things happen:

   1. I can mistake egotism for awareness. I believe that this is a danger in psychoanalysis, where understanding can remain on a verbal rather than a 'gut' level. I believe it is also implicit in some of the discussions of awareness in the Gestalt literature, where awareness can be taken as a verbalization of the 'sensation.' As I understand it, *any* self-statement of the kind "I am feeling hungry" is the exercise of egotism rather than of awareness in the Gestalt sense. It is an interruption to contact in that my awareness of the sensation of hunger will actually reduce as I pay attention to my verbalization. Once again, the act of verbalizing or egotising is not inherently problematic: If I have to perform complex acts in order to assuage my hunger (put aside work, go to the shops or a restaurant), then I will need to start in this way. However, once I mix up awareness and egotism, I am going to be unable to act spontaneously, and I would expect a Gestalt approach based on such verbal 'awareness' to inhibit spontaneity. In terms of conventional descriptions of psychopathology, this way of acting, when done habitually and without awareness, can be seen as 'schizoid,' withdrawal from relating and feeling into intellectual or fantasy activity.

   2. I can reify my subvocal speech, thinking and planning into a 'part of me' called **mind**. PHG speaks of mind as an 'unavoidable illusion' engendered by living in a 'chronic low grade emergency,' i.e. an environment where *every* situation is complex, so that, whenever I introspect, I am aware of these activities. I then regard this symbolic or thinking activity as having a life of its own, leading to such philosophical 'problems' as the relationship between mind and body. In a simpler environment, there would be no sense of ongoing 'mind,' but merely a need to think sometimes.

3. I will give to the egotism a flavor of whatever unfinished business is complicating the situation. For example, if I am expecting criticism and rejection from my environment, and therefore become habitually careful in my dealings with other people, my self-assessment in my egotism is likely to be self-critical and rejecting. This is my experience of clients with 'low self esteem,' and points to the inadequacy of therapeutic approaches which emphasize 'affirmation' or 'giving more positive introjects.' The point, as we shall see when we look at working with egotism, is to facilitate the client to rediscover the possibility of (and risk) much simpler and more direct relating to the environment. It is worthwhile once again emphasizing that the central core of Gestalt is experience at the contact boundary, not adjusting the 'internal' activities of the client. The assumption is that, as the client reengages at the contact boundary, the internal activities will necessarily change.

Working with habitual egotism

As with any habitual interruption to contact, the resolution is for the client to reconnect to here-and-now experience, starting with the experience in the therapy context, to discover what anxieties she brings to making this contact, and what possibilities are offered by making contact in a new way. Thus the client can come to decide afresh what contacts she is willing to engage in, and what to avoid.

Once again, I must not assume that the client will immediately accept my offer of moving out of egotism, even if it involves continual self-criticism. Any habitual behavior will have acquired an *ecological* importance in the way someone lives their life, and to drop any habit will disrupt that ecology. I am reminded of an article about workmates who talked to each other only while smoking, so that their relationship was disrupted by one of them stopping smoking. Rather, my aim is to bring that whole ecology into awareness, so that the client can decide whether to risk moving beyond the old ways to a new way of dealing with the possibilities and the anxieties.

I find that a useful way of bringing the wider field into the awareness of those who habitually egotise is to focus on simple sensory awareness, sometimes assisted by encouraging the clients to get massage for themselves. The client can then explore the anxiety that comes up as a result of acting out of pattern. I avoid intellectual discussion, including trying to argue the client out of very critical self-assessments. Those will tend to go in any case when the client reconnects with the environment, allows other people's evaluation of herself to be of interest, and is able to be authentically critical towards others.

Other Interruptions to Contact

There are many (sometimes heated) debates in the Gestalt world about what to include as basic interruptions to contact. Various writers have proposed new 'interruptions,' others have tried to reduce them to combinations of the 'more basic' ones, i.e. the ones mentioned in PHG. From what I have written above, it should be fairly evident that I do not see the interruptions as separate, but as supporting each other in various ways, e.g. the introjection of critical self-image in egotism, the projection of aggression in confluence. If this is the case, then it is difficult to sustain the view that they tend to occur only on specific and different situations. I am therefore happy to include the following additions to the list of interruptions to contact for their descriptive power, and in full awareness of the fact that they too will have links to other items on the list.

DEFLECTION

This is a term coined by Polster and Polster (1973), and is a form of what I call 'isolation.' In deflection, I push aside what comes to me, often in a covert way: Answering the question that is not quite the one asked, or pretending to listen but not listening.

Or I blunt the contact, for example by smiling when expressing anger. The contact boundary is not only impermeable, but greased! As with isolation, the person is not allowing himself the ego function of identification.

PROFLECTION

This is a term coined by Crocker (1981). It is when someone does to someone else what she wants that other to do to her, e.g. hugging someone when I want to have the other hug me, giving support when I am in need of support myself. I find this a useful template, and have added to my stock of experiments the one of reversing the arrow so that the client experiences receiving what s/he was giving out. A major aspect of proflection is projection of a need, but there is more than this: A kind of introjection of (identification with) the person I am seeking to fulfil the need. In any case, it is a common enough situation (particularly among people in 'helping professions') that it is worth having a simple term to denote it.

DESENSITIZATION

This term was introduced by Enright (1970). This is where I specifically numb myself to physical sensation, usually in response to an environment which is, or which I take to be, physically painful. Essentially this is a very tight, habitual focusing of awareness away from sensation, and one which allows very little sense of self in relation to other. It therefore usually goes along with narcissistic retroflection, used to provide a sense of self, and sometimes with habitual self-harmful behaviors (e.g. cutting oneself) both to provide some sensation, and to ritually cut through the barrier between me and not-me.

LEARNING TO INTERRUPT CONTACT

Some clients, especially those who have habitually moved into confluence and/or isolation, all or nothing, need to learn to use the more sophisticated interruptions to contact. For example, without the ability to project, it is impossible to be creative in the world. I need to first project my designs onto my environment, discover how they look there, and then I can go about making them real, whether that is in a work of art, a building, a job of work, or whatever. As another example, those who react impulsively will benefit from learning of the possibility of delaying their response by means of egotism, so that the response they finally produce is more skillful, and more accurate to their own needs and the needs of the situation. Those who always try and reinvent the wheel may benefit from introjecting what others have done for long enough to know what to assimilate and what to reject.

Having said this, for me one of the joys of working with clients who interrupt their contact at such an unsubtle, 'primitive' level (e.g. narcissistic and borderline clients) is the wonder with which they sometimes look at their world, almost like a newborn. I am reminded of the South American shamans who are prepared by being kept isolated in a cave for their first fourteen years, so that they never lose their sense of the wonder of their first view of the land and the people.

Chapter 6

CHILD DEVELOPMENT
AND PSYCHOPATHOLOGY

This chapter explores how we can integrate theories of child development and psychopathology into a relational, here-and -now Gestalt approach. This will inevitably be more technical and speculative than other chapters.

WHY STUDY CHILD DEVELOPMENT?

In the beginning, Perls was a contributor to psychoanalytic theories of child development. In fact, his first appearance as an innovative theorist was in his theory of the *dental phase* of child development (in "*Ego, Hunger and Aggression*"). Then, as the guru of the here-and-now at Esalen, Perls repudiated all that "elephant-shit," and what was important was the *obvious*, the therapeutic encounter. There was no need to study child development — it's all here now.

So, should we be studying child development at all? Is it all brought right here to the therapy relationship? *The approach that I take is that a moment of time has no significance in itself, but only in the context of the flow of time.* I have written about this previously as 'vector awareness.' For example, I am with a woman client who doesn't look at me and appears frightened of making contact. Is the client scared that I as a man may attack her (and in this case, why is she coming to a male therapist)? Is she scared rather that I might *not* attack her, so she would have to painfully reevaluate the world she lives in and her experiences to date? Do I remind her of somebody specific? Is she attracted to me and scared of showing the attraction? Or some combination of these? **The same event can have different meanings in different contexts.**

THE BIT THAT DOESN'T FIT WELL

Gestalt theory is centrally a *relational* and *process* theory: All events — including the intrapsychic — are given meaning by the relational (field) context and the ongoing process. Many of the child development theories from Freud onwards are *normative*: "this should be happening at this age, and be dealt with by this age." Furthermore, many psychoanalytic developmental theorists (notably *Margaret Mahler* (Mahler *et al*, 1975)) posit a period ("normal autism") when the child is out of contact with the environment, and a period ("symbiosis") when the child does not exist as a separate person from the mother.

Fortunately, more recent researchers and theorists, in particular *Daniel Stern* (1985), do not view the process of infant and child development in this way, but as an ongoing process involving several different strands which build on each other but are never complete. In fact, Margaret Mahler has taken these researches on board and moved from her better-known position to talking about the initial phase as "awakening" (cited in Stern p. 235).

In terms of the three boundaries I wrote of earlier (organism/environment, self/other and personality), my developmental history shows itself in two of them. Firstly, it shows in my *physical contact boundary*, who I am as a physical organism in relation to my environment: how my life up to now has contributed to my state of health and musculature, and the physical surroundings I find myself in, the people I am in contact with as friends or enemies, where I get (or don't get) food, love, sex, shelter. The other boundary is the *personality boundary*, who I take myself to be: My sense of myself and the world, the memories and myths by which I define myself. This will of course include my present understanding of my history and development. The third boundary, the self-other boundary, is not historical, but what we create here-and-now out of the present field, including the other two boundaries and their encapsulation of our history.

PERLS' FIVE LAYER THEORY OF DEVELOPMENT

Amazingly, Perls proposed his own theory of development, very similar to Stern's multi-strand approach, but about thirty years previously! However, I can only find one reference to this: A short part of a lecture Perls gave in 1957, reprinted in Perls (1978). It seems likely to me that it was a stepping-stone on the way to his better-known set of five layers of neurosis. However, it is quite distinct from the latter, and comes close to being a distinctive Gestalt developmental perspective. This theory shares with Stern the perspective of a number of phases of being and relating which build up sequentially, but which are never completed rather than the perspective of Mahler and others, where each phase starts on the completion of the previous one. In Perls' theory, the phases interact with each other, and we move between them. I want to present it in full, as it is not widely known, and complements well the approach I am taking.

Layer 1: 'Animal self'
This is the layer of 'little children, merely organic beings with their needs, their primitive functions, though often very differentiated functions, and their feelings.' (Perls 1978). Nothing more is said in the lecture about this layer, but we can see its

similarity to the 'id' in psychoanalysis, the 'Emergent Self' of Daniel Stern, or the 'Child Ego State' in Transactional Analysis. The work of Stern (1985) has shown how much potential autonomy can emerge within this layer very early on in an infant's development, and how soon it starts to link with a sense of 'core self.' However, remember that this layer does not end with the formation of successive layers: we can still operate from our basic needs, wants and feelings — although some people try and suppress these as 'infantile.'

Layer 2: The 'as-if' or 'social' layer

Here 'the loss of nature is replaced by the rules of games.' (Perls 1978). We learn to fit in with the rules of the society in which we live. Perls points out that we immediately invest less energy in our action if we are playing a role or obeying a rule than if our action arises out of an organismic 'animal' need. I do not fully agree with Perls here: I do not believe we lose energy if we make it *our* game, rather than a game played by other people's rules. It is 'natural' to play as-if games. But it does seem accurate to me to say that checking actions against the complex rules of family and society takes energy from the encounter.

Here, what Perls is talking about shows similarities to the psychoanalytic 'superego' or the Transactional Analysis 'Parent Ego State.' Its relationship to Stern is more obscure this time, since Stern does not particularly look at the infant in relation to society. However, the demands of society are there, if only in reflection in the socialization of the parents which impinges on the kind of birth the infant has, the physical, sensory and emotional contact they have with the infant, the patterns of feeding, and the patterns of contact with the wider community (including patterns of habitation: as a nuclear family, an extended family, or some more varied communal living style). All these will then affect how the infant relates to the world and to him/herself. Furthermore, Stern's category of 'core self' is in here somewhere, since, in the domain of 'core relatedness,' a major new factor is precisely this awareness of how we are seen by others.

The other aspect of this layer about which Perls does not speak here, is the inevitable clash between what the infant wants and what the world, especially parents, is willing or able to give. The baby experiences disappointments and frustrations as well as experiences of gratification of their needs and wants. Writers in Object Relations theory and Self Psychology (see e.g. Kohut, 1977) have written about the importance of these frustrations in the infant's development. Children at a very early age learn how to avoid the worst of the hurts and frustrations from their environment: this is the beginning of socialization. For example, Lakota Sioux babies in previous centuries had to learn quickly not to cry, as this might give away the tribe's position to an enemy (Hill, 1979).

Layer 3: The 'fantasy layer' or 'mind.'

Perls pointed to Freud's formulation of thinking as a 'trial act.' I visualize as a rehearsal for some complex action, or one where the consequences of some possible actions are significantly painful or desirable. For example, I would want to think about what I am going to say in an interview for a job I want, or as a defendant in court.

PHG has more to say about 'mind,' in a fascinating section. The authors write about 'mind' as an *unavoidable illusion* in a complex society which keeps us in a continuous sate of 'chronic low grade emergency.' In such a society, whenever we introspect, we become aware of ourselves thinking, and thus inevitably interpret this thinking as coming from a separate 'part' of ourselves. In a simpler society, much of our action would not need to be prefaced by thinking, and thus thinking would be merely one of the things we do. (Incidentally, given that this is how Perls understands 'mind,' his dictum "Lose your mind and come to your senses." becomes a much more interesting and complex idea than it is usually taken for!)

Of course, in any society our fantasy life also develops as an end in itself, especially in our dreams and stories. So in Australian aboriginal society, the split is not between mind and body, but between the material world and the 'dreamtime.' Both of these are experienced as important, and as informing each other.

Layer 4: The 'objectivation layer.'

'Here you tear sounds and tools out of their context and make them ready for a new organization.' (Perls 1978). Raw materials are made into tools, art, or artifacts, which are then kept in their made-up form. Metal and wood are made into a hammer, for example, and the object 'the hammer' is seen rather than the metal and wood. So the hammer stays as a hammer, and it is a rare person who will be able also to see wood for burning and a metal doorstop as further possibilities of the same matter. What de Bono calls 'lateral thinking' is basically an ability to put aside a particular 'objectivation,' and see things from a number of different, even contradictory, perspectives simultaneously.

Similarly, we 'objectify' sounds, and create words and tunes, which keep their meanings and significance for us. What all this amounts to is that we inhabit our world with complex, created objects (Freire calls them 'cultural objects'), not just simple, naturally occurring ones. Part of the gestalt of the complex object is its *use*, its *meaning*. Perls suggests to his listeners that they read Wittgenstein for more on the subject.

This 'objectivation' also underlies what Stern calls 'intersubjective relatedness,' where we come to know other people as being subjectivities like ourselves by objectifying our experiences as human beings, and recognizing these experiences in other people.

Layer 5: Organization of symbols and tools.

Now we learn to take the complexity even further, and go beyond tools to machines, beyond words to language, beyond tunes to musical form, beyond immediate community to 'society.' In the approach to 'self' which I have been discussing in this book, we can see the objectivation of 'self' and 'other' from the experience of contacting; and the organization of selves into Personality. We have formed our symbols into a symbolic world, whose contours we have named. This is the world of what Stern calls 'verbal relatedness.'

The coexistence of the layers

For Perls (1978), 'The essence of a healthy person is that there is a unity, an integration of all the layers; he does not live merely in one level . . . by integrating all these five layers we become truly ourselves, which means, we can discover the other, the world.'

So the vision underlying this model is of each level interacting with the others, with each needing to be available for full human functioning. In therapy, we can explore this interaction. Which level of the client's experience is relied on to the exclusion of which other? What are the implications for this in the client's life and contacting?

'NORMAL' AND 'ABNORMAL' DEVELOPMENT

The myth that goes with normative clinical theories of child development is that problems experienced in later life come from some failure of parenting. That is, there is some perfect model of parenting that would guarantee optimum, even prob-lem-free, functioning as the child becomes an adult.

Things are more complicated than this: The very aim to achieve perfection in child-rearing can interfere with the spontane-ous contact between parent and child, leading to, or deriving from, a narcissistic process. Surrounding children with a safe environ-ment can lead to a lack of 'street wisdom' which can cause problems in later life. A less normative way of looking at the relationship between parenting and later difficulties is that children will inevitably generalize from their early experiences, and make decisions about how the world is and how they are to interact with it.

There will be situations in adult life where these decisions are not appropriate or useful and leave someone unskilled to deal with what life brings. We can see particular patterns in this, some of which involve more serious difficulties than others: Neglect, physical and sexual abuse and continuous double messages from parents. A central point I want to make here is that the most severe difficulties are caused in situations where the child learns to *desensitize* and *deflect* in difficult situations (so they find it difficult to widen their boundaries if they need to), or where they do not learn to *desensitize* and *deflect* at all (for example, they are supposed to be permanently on the lookout for parents' distress). In neither of these cases do they learn to create a *permeable* boundary with their environment, which they can open and close at will. They will typically either find refuge in *isolation* or *confluence*.

I will say more about each of the above patterns:

NEGLECT

Neglect can be overt or covert. The aspect that I want to focus on here is that from the earliest time the infant needs to *see herself being seen* and responded to in a way that she can fit with what she has shown. Stern (1985) calls this 'matching.' If the child is neglected overtly, she will be mainly ignored, she won't be looked at, there will be no response to the child's distress. If the child is neglected covertly, the parents will go through the motions of contact, but since there is little contact the child will not experience being seen or responded to. There will be no matching that the child can use to gain a sense of her solidity. Covert neglect will also give a child a double message (see below) of neglect and acceptance. Other forms of neglect could be lack of food or misfeeding (including feeding babies by the clock); inadequate clothing, no parental figure to talk things over with (about difficulties in school, sex, etc.), overbusy or depressed parents.

A neglected child will either find the contact she craves from others, or, if that is not available, will create fantasy others to relate with, with all the problems inherent in 'narcissistic retroflection' which I discussed earlier. Examples I have come across include finding the needed other in the mirror, in a doll, or in television program characters who are adopted as 'parents.'

DOUBLE MESSAGES

Bateson et al. (1972) famously and controversially connect the development of schizophrenia with the *double bind*: Where parents give two opposite messages simultaneously in different modes to the child *and* the child is not allowed to make a meta-comment on the system (e.g. "Don't talk daft.") or to withdraw. Whether or not this is an 'explanation' of schizophrenia, these double binds certainly do occur in family communications. An example from a woman severely abused in childhood: Her mother complained that she didn't show affection to her. Her daughter said that she shouldn't be surprised after the childhood abuse. Mother replied (in a concerned tone of voice), "Those things didn't happen. If they really had, you'd be mad." Of course, if they hadn't she'd be mad anyway. There is a *subliminal* message "You're mad." and a message in the mother's tone of voice "I'm concerned for you." The child never knows where she is.

Another (and these days very frequent) example of this is the child whose parents believe that it is wrong to get angry with a child. What happens is that the child tests out limits by being 'naughty,' and is told at one level that what he has done is OK (in the name of encouraging the child's self-expression), but is aware (with the child's exquisite sensitivity) that the parent is furious and withdrawing to hide it. So the child tests out some more, and eventually the parent either lashes out or cuts off. In fact, the child's testing out has as its primary aim the provoking of a definitive action by the parents to resolve the double bind.

A third example is the parents who simultaneously give the messages "Don't come close" and "Don't move away" that I describe as an *oscillating family*. In such families, the child is either engulfed or abandoned, and never allowed to find a place of *contact* with the parents. Children in these families learn to fear both closing and widening of distance. As adults, with their own children, what becomes manifest is what I call 'reversal.' If the child wants the parent to move closer, the action she learns will achieve this is to move *away*. Conversely, to get the parent to move further away, the child moves *closer*. People who have learned this reversal will generally make relationships with others who act similarly, and have generally bizarre and mutually incomprehensible relationships with everyone else.

CHAOTIC AND NON-CHAOTIC UPBRINGING

This is a distinction which I find useful in therapy as a whole, and particularly when working with clients who have been abused. Clients whose childhood experience was of a chaotic upbringing, either unbounded or inconsistently bounded (e.g. they were punished randomly and quite inexplicably), usually bring that unboundedness and chaos to therapy. These are the clients whose intuitive response is often (self- and other-) destructive rather than helpful, and who will not know the difference between checking out the therapist and breaking the relationship. These clients need firm, consistent and contactful boundary-setting by the therapist. There is often a danger of breakdown, or acting out destructively in their relationships and job outside of therapy. It is unhelpful for someone to work on issues in therapy and at the same time have their partner leave or be sacked from their job (or end up on a psychiatric ward) because of their behavior in the world!

Other clients' childhood experience is of comparatively clear, consistent boundary-setting by parents — even if over-strict and violent. These clients are in many ways easier to work with, and find the process of therapy easier than chaotic clients. They are much more likely to be able to make good (or at least workable) decisions for themselves in therapy, and to be able to keep up their relationships and job while showing their anger and insecurities in therapy or other appropriate places. These clients can be allowed their head in therapy, and will usually use the freedom well (while being frightened of it).

GESTALT THERAPY AND PHYSICAL AND SEXUAL ABUSE

Gestalt therapy is very well-geared to working with people who have experienced abuse. We have the concept of *responsibility*, completely different to the concept of *fault*, so that we neither need to fall into the camp of "You've been abused so your life's ruined" nor "It's all your fault." We have a sophisticated analysis of the here-and-now, so we are not geared to uncovering traumatic scenes. I will speak in some detail about Gestalt work with people who have been abused, as it will illustrate very concretely how Gestalt therapy views the past and memory in relation to the present.

WHAT IS ABUSE?

I believe it is important to be clear what we mean by the term 'abuse.' Too often, it can become a badge to be worn in a victim culture, or a stick to beat parents with. Rather, I would reserve the term for situations where a child's body is used as an object on which an adult can act out his impulses, whether this is rage or sexual aggression. The essence of abuse is that the child is not treated as another human being, but, as clients have said to me, as a 'piece of meat.'

Parental violence as part of a human-to-human interaction, as punishment can often be, may or may not be damaging, but is experienced by the child completely differently, and to call it abuse muddies the waters, actually taking away from the terrible nature of abuse as I have defined it.

RESPONSE-ABILITY

Whatever happened in the past of the client, the client was *not* a passive victim. The child made choices (out of a limited range available), and decided how to respond to and understand the world. As time went on and the client grew older, the client made choices about whether and how to review these decisions. The *meaning* of the abuse now is the sum total of these choices, rather than the physical events per se.

Children who are being abused will almost always see it as their fault. I do not like to push "It was not your fault" too quickly with clients, as my experience is that clients do not cope well with this approach. Taking the blame is at least partly a *self-protective* measure, avoiding the need to say "There was nothing I could do to prevent the abuse." The idea that the child's parents would continue to abuse the child, and there wasn't any deficit in the child which she could correct and thus prevent the abuse, is usually too much for the child to accept. Furthermore, the client knows that she was not a passive 'victim,' but was making decisions, including very often the decision to split off from authentic functioning.

Working through this powerlessness and this decision to abandon authenticity involves experiencing *shame*, not just for what happened in childhood but for the repeats in adult life (either as victim or abuser). Very shame-filled areas include pleasurable sensations experienced during sexual abuse (not because they 'wanted it' but because bodies are made that way), abuse that was chosen by the child because it was the only contact available (a client told me "When I was raped at age 5 it was the first time anybody had loved me."), and where the child involved other children in the abuse. It will often take a long time before the client allows sufficient contact to be able to support experiencing this shame. Maybe more accurately, the client avoids this contact in order to avoid experiencing a level of shame which they imagine would be overwhelming. I shall say more about shame later in this chapter.

HERE-AND-NOW

Stated otherwise, from a Gestalt perspective, *the past does not exist!* What we bring from the past are memories (which may or may not be accurate), decisions, relationships, beliefs and attitudes. The here-and-now issue to do with memories of abuse (or non-memories where people have cut off from the memories) is "How do we use these memories in our life now?." The issue with decisions is "Do we need to redecide, and risk more pain?." The issue with relationships is "How do I (if at all) relate to these maybe elderly people who when I was little abused me, and who in doing so might have committed a serious criminal offence?."

A further issue is the context where either another parent knew about the abuse and did nothing about it (or participated), or had a relationship with the client where she did not feel able to tell the parent what was happening or did tell and was not believed. There will often be a lot of concealed anger towards that parent (often the mother, or could also be teachers or social workers) especially if the parent was otherwise loving. More would be expected of the loving parent than from the directly abusing one. The here-and-now issue could be a general expectation of not being supported; or difficulty in finding a satisfactory relationship to the unsupportive parent.

ABUSE AND BODIES

For clients who have been physically or sexually abused, bodies are a very sensitive issue. A good rule is "Don't touch if you even suspect abuse." As you increase your sensitivity, there may be situations in which it is right to touch, but if in any doubt, DON'T! This is *especially* true if the client's response to abuse has been to desensitize and repeatedly get into abusive situations: These clients will *expect* to be touched and won't argue, but somehow therapy will cease in any meaningful sense.

The major problem with touch is that it is a powerful language, and yet, for different people, the same touch may mean two very different things. I need to look out for situations in which I am saying one thing ("I am here with you."), while my client is receiving it as another ("Here's someone else who likes the feel of my body. Well, I'd better do what he wants, or he'll reject me.").

A good exercise when the client is ready is to ask them to look at parts of their body and just learn to accept the anxiety. This is a graded exercise, ranging from looking at a patch of skin on a hand, to taking all their clothes off (at home!) and looking at (or even touching) themselves.

ABUSE AND COUNTERTRANSFERENCE

The therapist's response to an abused client can take many forms:

Sadistic/punishing impulses, often encouraged by the client's ability to find the therapist's psychological weak spots. I have written above about *projective identification*, the therapist picking up feelings that originate with the client. You could see these impulses also as a form of projective identification with the client's own repressed anger and vengeance.

Over-protective impulses, where the client presents them-selves as not response-able for their lives. There is a limit to how much responsibility a therapist can take for a client's life outside the therapy situation, and where possible, clients must take that responsibility themselves. This is different from the situation where clients need to learn to accept support and help from another person. Clients who would benefit from this show themselves as self-contained rather than needy, and tend to avoid any support I might offer.

Sexual fantasies

I might experience sexual fantasies towards clients who have been abused. They will sometimes act in a very seductive manner towards the therapist or other group members. Once the relationship between therapist and client is strong enough, these (and punishing fantasies) can be owned by the therapist, with the rider that " . . . and I will not hurt you or have a sexual relationship with you." It is worth realizing that clients who have been sexually abused will usually be able to tell if someone is sexually attracted to them, and it will be a factor in the relationship whether the therapist mentions it or not.

Coping with countertransference

Two skills are needed in order not to become confluent with the strong countertransference with these clients: *Awareness* and *acceptance*. I need to be *aware* of my impulses, even/especially the ones that are not 'nice.' I need to be able in my own therapy or supervision to look at my part in them. I also need to be able to *accept* all these impulses. There is an element of parallel process here: If someone believes that certain impulses are *in themselves* signs that the person is evil or unacceptable, they will often respond by saying "Well if I'm evil and unacceptable, this is what bad people do, so this is what I'll inevitably do." This will either be done overtly, or by splitting, with the "bad person" disowned and split off, but acting covertly. Either of these could be the client's experience with an abusing parent. In the same way, I as therapist need to be able to incorporate a sense of my whole range of impulses, both noble and otherwise.

'FALSE MEMORY SYNDROME'

This is an attempt to put a Gestalt perspective to a debate that is attracting a lot of attention in the psychotherapy world, and in the world beyond psychotherapy as well, raising questions about the value and possible dangers of psychotherapy.

The question is this: How reliable is memory? In particular, if, during the course of therapy, the client remembers scenes of childhood abuse, is this memory a reliable rendering of what actually occurred? This is particularly significant in the case of child sexual abuse, since, first of all, such abuse is a serious criminal offence, with the potential for an abuser to suffer imprisonment; secondly, an allegation of such abuse will almost always have a traumatic effect on the relationships within a family and a community. There are few areas where the effects of therapy will have such an immediate and far-reaching effect on the client and those around her.

Thus the underlying concerns are twofold: On the one hand, what if the memories are inaccurate, and someone is falsely accused of a serious crime against a child, and wrongly suffers imprisonment or ostracism; on the other hand, what if the specter of false memory is used by abusers to protect themselves and to repeat the childhood experience of not being believed? Three very different systems are potentially clashing: The therapeutic, the family and the legal.

In such a situation, the role of the therapist rightly comes under intense scrutiny. Where does the image of abuse come from originally: The therapist or the client? Are there situations where the therapist makes the assumption that abuse occurred to explain what the client is doing? Can certain behavior only be explained by a history of abuse? An even wider question is: Does remembering and reliving an experience of abuse correlate with healing for the client?

So from our first question about the reliability of memory come a large number of very serious questions, up to and including whether psychotherapy is in itself harmful.

What is memory?

The first point that we need to acknowledge is that one common image of memory as a tape recording is totally inaccurate. Modern memory research (see in particular Rossi (1986)) shows that memory is a part of a **state-dependent system of memory,**

learning and behavior (SDMLB). What this means is that memories are associated with a particular emotional or physical state, so that this state can call them up, whereas in another state they might not be able to be remembered. For example, something memorized when drunk might not be remembered when sober, but recalled when once again drunk. A stressful experience will be remembered better at a time of stress (just when we least need it!). Furthermore, memory thus raised is actually *created* at the moment of the raising, and that some details will be experienced differently at different moments of recall.

The physical and emotional state at the time of recall will also be incorporated into the state dependent system. Thus, ten witnesses to a crime or an accident will give ten different descriptions of the event. The act of telling, say, a policeman (or a therapist) will often solidify a particular memory which might not otherwise have been so solid. This is in fact part of the explanation of how therapy works. A client brings a state-dependent memory involving stress and insufficient safety or support to a therapeutic situation where they also know that they are safe and supported: This experience of trust gets incorporated into the state-dependent system, which is thus not so overwhelmingly stressful. Their learning about the world and behavior in the world will also change as the state-dependent system changes.

Can a therapist induce false memories?

The answer to this is: Of course! If a client comes to any professional wanting help, she usually has a mindset to accept what that professional says, especially if it powerfully explains the problems they experience. I have myself experienced false memories during my hypnotherapy training: On checking on the accuracy of early childhood memories, I found they were not accurate. Gestalt in particular talks about the co-creation of meaning in relationship, of the inaccessibility of the past in itself and of memory being a present event arising in the relationship to our environment. Thus Gestalt fits very well with theories of SDMLB. We must also acknowledge, however, that it puts a question mark over the idea of 'facts,' which are a central concern in the legal process.

Thus a female client comes to see a therapist suffering from fear during sexual intercourse, dreams of rape, fear of men and few memories of childhood. It is very easy to assume that this client has been sexually abused as a child and has repressed the memory. This assumption would then influence the future actions of the therapist, and can support the formation of false memories of abuse for the client. This is true even if the client has been abused! One of the potential problems of any interpretation is that it can be essentially accurate, and still be introjected by the client, separating her from her own experience. To get even more specific, the client may have had experience of abuse, which the therapist believes was carried out by the client's father. However, the abuse may have happened with someone else entirely: Uncle, babysitter, brother, etc.

The therapist may be encouraging the client to develop visual memories. Such memories are reconstructed each time they are recalled. Sometimes it would be impossible for there even to be visual memories of abuse: When the room is dark, when the child has her eyes shut or covered, when she is face down (say in anal abuse). The memories would be in physical sensations or emotions rather than pictures. Yet clients do 'recall' pictures in situations where those pictures are not likely to be direct memory. And sometimes those pictures present accurate information. One man after therapy confronted his father with an accusation of abuse in infancy: The father immediately agreed that he had done it. However, it is important to bear in mind that memories 'recovered' by people under hypnosis or suggestion are both more vivid and more likely to be inaccurate than memories recovered without suggestion.

Another situation where a person can develop false memories is where one parent's actions are redefined by the other parent as a hostile gesture. For example, if a father is physically affectionate towards a daughter, the mother, who is in dispute with the father, or jealous of his relationship with his daughter, can tell the daughter there is something 'perverted' about such contact. If the daughter takes the mother's side in the parental conflict, she may come to agree that the father has abused her. If she confronts him with accusations of abuse, she locks herself out of a relationship with him, and locks herself out of being able to see the difference between physical affection and assault!

Is 'False Memory Syndrome' a cover under which abusers can hide themselves?

Again the answer is: Of course. It would be incredible if people who had been abusing their children didn't hide under the banner of 'False Memory,' and indeed one of the founders of the American False Memory Association has been found to be involved with child pornography. In talking about the ways in which false memories can be produced in therapy, I am not saying that memories of abuse are all (or even mostly) false, or that they should not be producible in court. The problem of the relationship of memory to facts is a general legal problem, which usually gets resolved reasonably acceptably. What I am saying is that therapists need to give at least as much care to the responsibility involved in interpretation in the case of sexual abuse as to any other, and be aware of the limitations of memory, the potential for truly messing up the lives of the client and her family, and of strengthening the hand of those who would have us believe that it is all false memory.

Is it necessary for the client to remember?

Another contribution Gestalt has to make is in its emphasis on **present-centeredness** and field theory. Except in the case of a resulting permanent physical injury, there is no *direct* connection between what happened in childhood and how someone is now. What does affect a person's present functioning is an accumulation of: Learnings and understandings about the world, often beginning in childhood; splits in personality and repressions of aspects of experience in order to psychically survive overwhelming experience ('unfinished business'); a sense of 'no-one will believe me' or 'I'm dirty'; a devaluation of one's own needs and an overconfluence with other people's needs. It is in the context of this field that I would like to look at the question of the healing potential of remembering what has been forgotten. The question for me is "What is the present significance of a client remembering something with me?"

I want to distinguish two situations: Where a client tells me something he has never forgotten, but hasn't told people; and where a client remembers something that he didn't know that he knew at the start of therapy. As I implied above, I'm excluding the situation where I suggest that a client was sexually abused: I just don't do that. (At best it would short-circuit the client's own remembering and telling me; at worst it could be a false interpretation of what I notice about the client, and one the client then starts to believe.) In the first situation, the significance is whatever is significant to the client in telling me now. This might be challenging an injunction not to tell or a threat about the consequences of telling anyone. It might be an assertion that "I will be heard and believed." It may be a statement of trust of the therapist and/or a group. It may be a recognition of adulthood: Times have changed.

The second situation is when, during the course of a therapy, a client *without prompting* (direct or indirect) remembers events. I regard memories in such a context as being as reliable as any other memory. That is, it may not be reliable: The client may not be telling the truth; the client may have some inability to separate fantasy from memory; the client may be passing on an interpretation from someone else (including a previous therapist); the memory may have become radically changed in the interval since the actual events.

But this is the normal course of events which both therapists and the courts have to live with and deal with. As an experienced therapist, I will be making my own assessment of the reliability of what the client is saying and of their reality testing. Is the client given to flights of fancy? Is she repeating something told to them by someone else? Does the client have some intended gain from telling me? I am aware that sometimes clients get some advantage out of telling a particular story to anyone who will listen (even if the story's true!). This is all part of my responsibility. If a client goes to court with abuse allegations, the court will be making similar determinations, often on the basis of less knowledge. The here-and-now significance will be of a dawning realization that the contact with the therapist offered here is different — safer, more accepting, more attuned to the client's needs, more willing to listen — than she would have considered possible.

Considerations for the therapist

The therapist has an ethical responsibility to be aware to the best of her ability of the potential pitfalls in any intervention she makes. In the specific case of the possibility of a history of sexual abuse as a child, I would suggest these as the main responsibilities of the therapist:

Under no circumstances to be the first to suggest to the client that he might have been sexually abused. This cannot be helpful **even if it is true**, for the reasons I have given above.

To take as central the present personhood and needs of the client rather than taking as central the events of the past, however traumatic. Not to assume that the remembering of childhood abuse is in and by itself healing.

To be aware of the circumstances in which a client might misremember or pretend a memory of abuse: Poor reality testing, so that she cannot tell the difference between a fantasy and a reality; to get some personal gain; to please someone else, including the therapist; because it might have powerful explanatory power and make incomprehensible facets of their life comprehensible. Not to push for visual memories which are possibly not there.

To believe and support the client within the boundaries above, and not to give the client less or more belief or support because of the therapist's own countertransferential response to a particular experience like child abuse. The client should not be subliminally influenced by positive or negative reinforcement to talk on a particular subject.

To be aware of the different requirements of the therapeutic and the legal process, and of family dynamics. Not to assume that to tell the courts or family members will be a healing act. Those decisions will carry great risks which don't usually fall on the therapist but on the client, and must therefore be decided on freely by the client.

Not to be swayed by emotional arguments for or against the reality of memories of child sexual abuse. Each client is different, and no general argument covers these differences.

In the next chapter, I will look at how this Gestalt approach to the self and child development relates to work with 'self disorders.'

Chapter 7

SELF DISORDERS

I start this section with an excerpt from a client's letter to me (used with the client's permission, for which my thanks). I have added the italics to illustrate a process which I will speak about more in this chapter: Self becoming more stable through relationship with the therapist, leading to self-acceptance, even her fragility:

●

Any sense of connection/being interested/involved = I want to scream

Peter:
First, I want to thank you for your believing in me — when I find it hard to believe in myself, and for accepting me as I am.

2 days later

I think I had some more energy outwards after talking with you on Monday. I could accept my sense of dream state when with people, and was surprised at my involvement. I felt very raw, as if I had no skin and I felt very shaky and my legs weak and limited ability to think — *but I could accept all this changing, varying being.*

I don't mean to take away from anyone else or compare myself. But I have had some very long, continuous and intermittent nightmarish times in the last few years — with incredible, for me, feelings of non-existence and inability to communicate, and know, where I am. I seem to, perhaps, be getting more accustomed to the feelings — maybe?

I don't know how to feel real just at the moment and when I looked in the mirror earlier I couldn't see me anywhere. My face and body look like a stranger with no inside.

Dare I read any of this to you, Peter? Can I cope with being in the open?

I need to do something because I cannot even partly relax into being at the moment — *I'm so tired* of holding on to my self, of *being on hold.*

It is important to me to talk to you about me. On Monday I thought "it was right" to be moving towards "light" — not right to dwell on feeling powerless and lost.

Having tried to work towards "light," which was fine and good for bringing me round, *I afterwards felt I don't have to be moving anywhere. I need to acknowledge me as I am.*

Some of my numbness and distancing is to do with not moving on, getting involved, until I acknowledge and accept my painful self — until I accept I have suffered and am suffering and I am very frightened of being alive. Some of the numbness is keeping at bay the inclination to go crazy and scream and "freak out." *I feel as if my inside body is contracting and keeping me very still for fear of falling in, in little pieces* and being sick and feeling very ill and weak.

I so want to scream. But my body hurts too much at the moment. Inside indigestion pains and stiffness of legs, knees, neck, mouth. I feel like stopping breathing. Feeling part of my surroundings seems lost forever. I'm so rigid. I hurt so much.

(and a voice tells me I'm so self-centered and very lucky). And I want to scream and scream and scream.

Today, I felt I could accept my limits (and numbness) which I understood as connected somehow to my fear.

I feel like I'm holding myself together and it's taking all my energy.

●

THE GESTALT ORIENTATION

The orientation of Gestalt therapy is a *relational* one. We do not primarily look either inwards — at drives, introspection, self-awareness — nor outwards — towards a stimulus 'causing' a response, sociology, the demands of the environment 'making' us be a certain way. What we explore is the process of the person relating to her environment on the basis of organismic needs, demands from the environment, and our choices and interests. And in this process, *self* is actualized. Self is seen not as a thing, but as a polar creation in relation to *other*. Neither concept is meaningful except in relation to its polar opposite. Thus this process of contacting and relating on the basis of needs and interests *is* self.

ALL NEUROSIS AND PSYCHOSIS IS SELF-DISORDER

With this basis, one can see all disorders of this basic contacting process as disorders of self. Some forms of relating between organism and environment are being avoided, leading to needs being unsatisfied, interests being repressed, and the free and lively flow of the interchange between organism and environment interrupted. This is the basis of what PHG calls the 'autonomous criterion' of health:

> When the figure is dull, confused, graceless, lacking in energy (a 'weak gestalt'), we may be sure that there is a lack of contact, something in the environment is blocked out, some vital organic need is not

127

being expressed; the person is not 'all there,' that is, his whole field cannot lend its urgency and resources to the completion of the figure (PHG).

Also with this basis, we are talking about a self which is inherently fragile. Thus, rather than looking at how self developmentally becomes fragile, we would be exploring the ways in which we work to *stabilize* the self, and the difficulties we might encounter in doing this.

The three forms of self process which I want to particularly look at are *id*, *ego* and *personality*. Each of these contributes in its own way towards both healthy functioning, and towards particular types of unhealthy functioning.

ID

This is defined as that part of the contacting process where all is potential. Nothing has particularly caught my interest, I have no particular needs, and I am open to myriad potential contacts. In terms of figure-ground, my experience is of fleeting figures emerging from a ground pregnant with possibilities. I will be particularly open to bodily awarenesses and to the unexpected from my environment, but am not at present identifying with any of these.

If I do not allow this stage of the contacting process, I will find it impossible to go on to identifying needs and interests, and the resources in the environment through which these needs and interests can be met. At an extreme, id disorders are psychotic, "the annihilation of some of the givenness of experience" (PHG). Here I want to focus on two aspects of avoidance of the id stage of contacting. The first is that a major purpose of this avoidance is the control of *uncertainty* and *spontaneity* — of fragility, if you like. If I start my contacting process on the basis of my formed preconceptions rather than immersion in what is there, I can get a sense of having tamed the world and made it an extension of my own fantasies or ideas. The second aspect has an opposite effect. If my environment is impoverished, lacking possibilities which match my physical or emotional needs, I can invent a fantasy world which I can use to nourish myself.

Non-psychotic forms of id disorder are the *schizoid* and *narcissistic* personality disorders. In the schizoid process, openness to experience, which I reject as too anxiety-provoking, is replaced by a cognitive relating to the verbalized or symbolized world. In the narcissistic process, I experience the environment as too dangerous or impoverished to contact. I therefore split myself, and retroflectively experience self in the contact across the split rather than with the environment. I would also put here the obsessive-compulsive disorders (OCD). In these, the existential anxiety of relating is moderated by some activity (e.g. hand-washing, cleaning, avoiding condoms) whose main function is to be more controllable than the openness to experience in the id process. I find the 'feel' of clients with OCD very similar to, and often coupled with, the 'feel' of narcissistic or schizoid process.

WORKING WITH ID DISORDERS

Looking at these disorders in this way, it seems to me to follow that their 'treatment' is to invite the client to reopen to contact: Bodily awareness, sensory awareness, simple human to human meeting, and to avoid acting out any more complex agenda until this has been achieved. Unfortunately, the anxieties involved in the choice to live this way mean that the achievement of this openness takes a long time. Any attempt by the therapist (or by a client trying to 'be a good client') to rush the process will result in the client acting in a number of different — but all destructive — ways: Leaving therapy; acting compliantly and in the process splitting off further; or acting out destructively, either towards self or towards others, e.g. by getting into a damaging relationship, stopping eating, washing hands till they bleed, drinking heavily.

My image is of standing close to the client (but not too close), holding out my hand to invite contact, and not otherwise moving any closer. The client then chooses any closing of the distance between us.

Example

Jenny is sitting as she often sits, eyes lowered, making very little movement, and not speaking.

P: Would you be willing to glance at me for a moment, then look away?
J: (Glances up, then winces) I feel scared when I look at you.
P: Is there anything you see of me that you feel scared of?
J: You look angry to me.
P: I have no awareness of feeling angry. What do you see in my face that you interpret as anger?
J: You're not smiling.

In this extract, I am encouraging visual awareness, and awareness of what meaning Jenny is making of what she sees. I might also ask Jenny to tell me how she pictures me when she doesn't look at me, and compare it with how she does see me.

I associate this looking down, not moving with the experience of shame. I will write more later on this theme.

NEUROSIS/LOSS OF EGO FUNCTIONS

Ego is the active process of moving towards some aspects of the environment ('identification') and away from others ('alienation'): that is, the formation of figure and ground in the service of contacting the environment in a nourishing way. From the preponderance of ground in the id process, with transitory figures emerging and then retreating to ground, I now identify with and move towards ('aggress' towards) a particular need or interest, and a particular aspect of the environment which is interesting or might satisfy my need. Thus 'identification' and 'alienation' are called the 'ego functions.'

If I feel sufficiently frightened about the potential consequences of this aggression from previous experience, I will not be willing to form a nourishing contact-boundary with my environment. In particular, with other people, I will find it difficult to identify, or commit to a stable relationship; and I will also find it difficult to alienate, or end a relationship with grace or negotiate a change in the relationship. I will then either cling to or avoid other people, or — in the case of borderline personality disorder — split my process and alternate between the two.

My understanding of the developmental etiology of borderline personality disorder follows the approach of James Masterson (1981). His schema is:

Separation/Individuation ⇒ *depression* ⇒ *defense.*

That is, the basic need for the child to assert her individuality (via the ego functions) is disrupted by the parent's wish to cling to the child, and/or to experience rage and reject him/her if she moves away. The conflict and despair the child feels in this circumstance is too overwhelming, so she defends against it by splitting the clinging ('rewarding') parent and the child's confluence-seeking personality from the rejecting ('withdrawing') parent and the child's angry, rejecting personality. Thus when the borderline client is in one of these states, she blocks off awareness of the possibility of the other.

Again, given this understanding, the important factors in working with clients who have given up ego functions are *contact* and *choice*. It is particularly important to separate emotion and choice, since, in the absence of choice, the simplest way to decide what to do is to become confluent with one's emotions: If I feel it, I do it. My understanding is that we have no choice about or responsibility for our emotions: They are our raw energetic response to our environment. Our choice and our response-ability is in how we act, whatever we feel. This is often felt as a real liberation by people whose family introject is that feeling and doing are the same. These clients are much more robust than id-disordered clients, and I can actively offer relationship, and set boundaries round the acting-out which could wreck our relationship. I also act, with borderline clients, as the guardian of the out-of-awareness polarity. Thus when the client sees me as rejecting and becomes angry, I remind him that we have also been close; and also vice versa. What is *very dangerous* is to simply reflect back the client's experience, especially of the angry rejecting pole, since the client does not have the perspective to avoid slipping towards a pit of rage and pain which could lead to suicide, or towards the client leaving therapy, relationships, job, accommodation, etc.

The other important point to note is that the client often does not feel better for the good work that we do together: He feels the depression/despair/grief that the loss of ego functions avoided. This is the 'impasse' and 'implosion' that Perls (1969) referred to in his 5-layer model of neurosis. The client will need a great deal of support through this stage.

PERSONALITY FUNCTION

This is the verbal sense of 'who I am,' 'how I act.' It positively provides much of our sense of continuity of self, and avoids us having to reinvent the wheel each time we act. Negatively, each use of personality rather than ego/choosing involves a loss of choice.

If we decide a lot of our actions on the basis of personality, through introjects or desire for perfection, there will be many situations where we find it very difficult to act usefully: We will be very limited in our ways of acting and relating. We are in the 'role-playing layer' (Perls, 1969), or the 'as-if' layer (Perls, 1978): Rigidly identified with a particular image of ourselves.

The therapist can respond by providing experimental situations where the role does not work, to provide a safe environment where the client can experiment with new ways of acting, and thus an expansion of self -possibilities.

SHAME

Shame is an acknowledgment of having offended against my selfhood by separating from my needs out of fear. For me shame and its less powerful cousin embarrassment are the emotions associated with the move out of a limited neurotic self to a more contactful, choiceful self, but is also experienced where I feel it is too dangerous to 'be myself.'

I am aware that there has been much thinking in the Gestalt world on the subject of shame (see for example the *British Gestalt Journal*, vol. 4, no. 2 for a series of papers). My concern here is to look at the composition of the shame-experience for the client who experiences it rather than the actions of the environment which would be likely to precipitate the shame, for it is the client, his experiences, and his side of the interaction which is actually present in the therapy (see below for when the therapist — or group member — triggers shame). Here as elsewhere, I take as central to Gestalt therapy that there is no non-responsible partner in the interaction, no "innocent victim." In fact, I believe that to regard someone as such is a collusion in a depowering process.

Theoretically, I would understand shame as *retroflection of the disgust reflex*. "Disgust" is discussed by Perls (1947) in *Ego, Hunger and Aggression*:

> Disgust means the non-acceptance, the emotional refusal of food by the organism proper, whether the food be *really* in the stomach or throat, or only *imagined* to be there . . . This kind of resistance belongs to the class of annihilation . . . An additional resistance, a *resistance against resistance*, is of special importance: the repression of disgust.

Thus, if I find it impossible to maintain my 'emotional refusal' or alienating of something I am being 'force fed,' because of overwhelming force, fear of rejection, or lack of perspective, I will both repress and retroflect my disgust. Disgust then becomes self-disgust, annihilation becomes self-annihilation, alienation becomes self-alienation.

My experience of working through such self-alienation is that clients often experience nausea, or show facial expressions indicating disgust, as they work through this material. The therapist must be willing to be available to receive the client's disgust and rage, as it is directed outward, without backing away.

It is not my task as a therapist to avoid a client feeling shame or embarrassment: It is often a sign that new possibilities are emerging. However, I need to be aware how distressing such feelings can be. What is important is that I do not push clients so fast that they are flooded with shame beyond their self-support, or their ability to use their contact with me and the rest of their environment for support. Some writers, influenced by Self Psychology, have suggested that a client feeling 'shamed' is a therapeutic mistake. In a sense this is true: If they feel 'shamed,' it means they do not feel in a position to own their own shame. The point is to grade contact and speed of working so that clients can feel ownership of their own emotions, including shame.

In the next chapter, I will make an attempt to illustrate the thinking of this and the previous chapter with a story about the development of the fictitious client Jan, whom I introduced earlier.

Chapter 8

JAN'S STORY

In this chapter, I will illustrate my own approach to child development and self disorders with this story of my fictional client Jan, based on the research on the world of the infant by Stern (1985). I find Stern's thinking highly compatible with both Gestalt theory and my observations of my own children when they were babies and young children.

•

Jan was born 35 years ago. Her immediate experience was of adaptation to a new situation with new dynamics: Having to breathe, maintain temperature, adjust the amount of light entering her eyes, and deal with her hunger reflex, nappies, clothes, baths: A suddenly wider and more exciting and frustrating sensory environment than that of the womb. Some of her responses were already in place — 'hard wired.' She looked for nipples and faces rather than other sights, human voices rather than other sounds. She had not a fully formed memory, but she could learn, and immediately started making some sense (non-verbal, of course) of the sights, sounds, smells and physical contacts of her environment. She could do some 'cross modal matching' (Stern, 1985): Connect a sound with a person, a sight with a feel or a smell.

It is also important for us to be aware how *little* was 'hard-wired' for Jan at birth. Most animals are born with instinctual responses to a large number of the situations they might meet. They make choices, but, in the main, the bases for their choices are instinctual. The impact of this can be seen in the fact that human beings adopt a set of *values*, and that these values can be very different for different people. These chosen values, and the other relatively invariant ways of dealing with contacts in the environment which are called the personality function of self, then form the basis for our specific choices. What is more, Jan will be able to update her personality and values over time.

Jan could remember, and therefore learn, but her remembering was very different to her (and my) remembering now, for several reasons. Firstly, the physiology underlying her memory was not fully mature, and will continue maturing till about the age of five. We are not clear what form memory would have taken for Jan in infancy. We know that some form would be present, sufficient for the large amount of learning that she had to do. We know that this learning forms a continuum of maturation which started before birth, by, for example, the signs of recognition babies of a certain generation gave to the theme tune of 'Neighbors,' the soap opera many mothers-to-be watched while pregnant.

The second way in which Jan's infant memory was different to how we would experience memory was in the fact that Jan did not have words. One of the ways adults remember is by a parallel world of words which symbolize our experiences, and by which we can communicate them to others, and to ourselves as if we were another person. Jan did not at the time have that available to her, and I would imagine her experience of memory more as recognition, or a sense of *deja vu*.

Thirdly, Jan would not have had (but would slowly be developing), a sense of what I would call the *mechanisms* of the world. The brown thing falling on Jan in the pram would not be a leaf falling from a tree because it is autumn which I have seen before . . . Or, this light is the sun, this is the bedroom light. Events are much more in and for themselves, and less part of a known skein of interactions. I imagine that along with this would go a much greater sense of wonder, and greater levels of emotion. Hunger would not be connected with anticipation of a meal, but with panic if food is not immediately forthcoming. The meal would be total satisfaction, rather than something to be fitted in between appointments.

What I want to get across, along with the factual statements, is a sense of the *alienness* of Jan's memory experience, even though it is an alien experience we have all been through. However, any memory experience we might have of this time would be filtered through our different physiology, understanding and verbiage. It is like the science fiction stories about the memories of an alien species being implanted into the brain of a human being, who cannot make the same sense of them that the alien could. What is more, memory is not like a tape recording of what happened, but a construct, as I have discussed earlier.

For our purpose now, we can say that Jan was remembering, matching experiences, and learning. A lot of this learning was necessarily passive: In Gestalt terms, a lot of her self process was id. Her body 'looms large' (PHG), her connection to any one aspect of experience would have been fleeting and hallucinatory. A few things would have become figural (ego): Breasts when she was hungry (and probably in a hard-wired way at other times), lights, things (like cot toys) which she recognized, and maybe was learning to manipulate. She was developing (non-verbal) communication with those around her, patterns of linked behaviors with mother, father, brother, where the actions of one prompted the corresponding action of the other (clutching a finger which is offered, for example). This is a kind of *language* without words, and it is only through the prior ability for this kind of communication that words can be learned, and verbal communication can develop.

And here problems started. Jan's mother and father had been brought up by parents very similar to how they now were.

Their early experience had been of very little touch, and they did little touching of Jan. Jan's recognition patterns of bodily experience, by which she developed her sense of herself as a physical person, did not include loving holding. They included some rough handling, not at this stage with any intent to hurt, but through lack of parental sense of the impact of different types of touch on sensitive skin. She also experienced sensations of dirty nappies left on too long, so they rubbed painfully against her bottom and genital area. Jan's part in all this was to lower her own sensitivity to rough handling. She was not shocked by these experiences: In one way they were part of the patterns of recognition which for her, as for all infants, were a kind of security. She certainly cried less than a baby who rarely experienced painful handling. It was in the roughness of these contacts that she learned to know herself as a physical being.

All this is the functioning of what Daniel Stern called *emergent self*. Stern's four domains of self start sequentially, and continue throughout life. Like the Gestalt definition of self, they are all defined relationally. I would associate emergent self experience in later childhood and adulthood with Gestalt therapy's definition of the id process of self.

I will now continue Jan's story into the development of Stern's next domain of selfhood and relatedness: core self.

Jan has got to four months old. Physically she has grown and developed. She can, as Gestalt says, *aggress* on her environment much more. Her movements are often purposeful, made with some expectation of the result of those movements. These expectations are still not verbalized, of course, but recognized and remembered patterns, of which Jan has taken charge. She even recognizes an increasing number of words that people round her say, and associates them as part of the patterns (while not having the vocal control or practice to respond verbally herself — as Jan gets older, this combined understanding and inability increasingly becomes a source of frustration to her). She wants, and works for, attention. Thus, when the woman next door says "Who's a pretty girl?" in a certain tone of voice, Jan knows that certain movements will get her more friendly attention.

When Jan's mother says "No!," she knows two scenarios, both of which she uses at one time or another. If she continues doing exactly what she has been doing, the volume of mother's voice would increase, and Jan would feel the painful sensation of a slap or a shaking. This would be attention, and a physical affirmation of her physical being, but still unpleasant and somewhat frightening. However, the unpleasantness and the tinge of fear (reduced by the knowledge from previous occasions that her survival isn't threatened) are also reassuringly familiar to Jan. Sometimes she has reduced her sensitivity to physical sensation so much that she does not even feel a more gentle touch from the neighbor. At other times, Jan would be in less need of attention, for example if she's sleepy, and then she knows that responding to mother's "No!" with quietness and physical stillness will usually make mother more silent and less pain-inducing.

These patterns of behavior are reproduced similarly with her father and brother. When her brother Simon (six years older) starts experimenting with her genitals, her experience is very mixed. It is attention, it is often less unpleasant than other things Simon sometimes does — and is even pleasurable, similar to what Jan has done to herself even from before birth. The other confusing thing is Simon's reaction. He seems uncomfortable doing it, and once is caught by father and beaten in front of Jan. At least mother is comfortable when she shouts and slaps Jan.

Jan's father is not around very much. When he is around, he sometimes sits her on his knee and reads her a story. He feels to Jan just as uncomfortable doing this as her brother does in his contact with her. She is also frightened of his size and strength. He has slapped her once or twice, but, more to the point, she has also seen him beat Simon much more severely. This is much more terrifying to her, since she doesn't know what actions of hers might precipitate father beating her, and has no way of quantifying what that would be like, whether she would survive, and how much it would hurt. Jan is therefore very still when her father is around, and father congratulates himself that this 'goodness' has been achieved without him shouting at her, or hitting her hardly at all. He can see himself as an indulgent father of a daughter who is much better behaved than Simon (but boys will be boys). He rather looks down on his wife, who can't seem to 'handle' Jan like he does: She seems to cry a lot when looked after by her mother. He says "Who's daddy's best girl?", in a tone of voice to which Jan knows how to respond from prior experience with the neighbor.

In Jan's more active choosing and interacting, we can see the development of her ego functions of identification and alienation. In fact, she has to some extent alienated her id process of uncommitted openness to the environment. The environment is no longer just a source of wonder, but also of threat and unpleasantness. She focuses on potential sources of threat, and dulls her sensitivity to sensation. Not all the time: She *is* loved by her parents, who show it in the way that is possible for them, and she loves them as well, in much the same way. Jan has no doubts that she will be fed, clothed, kept warm and clean, protected from external dangers (the dog who barked at her and was shooed away, even Simon being pulled off when he hurt her). She has toys, sometimes mother or father or Simon play with her, and she rediscovers her delight in her playful contact with the world. Sometimes other toddlers come and play with her, sometimes she goes to a childminder and plays with other children. This is not a caricatured bleak existence. Her major fears are not about things that have happened to her, but about things she fears happening, especially with father, and which, paradoxically when they do happen, when he does beat her when she's older, become less frightening, since pain in itself is familiar to her.

Jan is now certainly developing *personality*. She does not put it into words, but knows herself to be a 'good girl' with father, and that his part is to tell her so with his tone of voice, the words that she is increasingly recognizing, and by relaxing with her. He has told men friends that Jan is "the only woman in his life who doesn't give me earache." In her recognition of this concept of herself, Jan actually gets angry with her father when he is away, or unfriendly towards her, but in a careful, controlled way. I suppose we could say that her personality function was a 'verbalized' understanding of herself in an action language shared between herself and her father.

With mother, Jan has achieved a more businesslike relationship. She no longer needs mother's attention so much, and is fairly quiet with her to avoid her anger. This is a good thing for Jan, since mother is somewhat jealous of how well her husband gets on with his daughter. She is also ashamed of this, and doesn't often take her feelings out on Jan. Simon still teases Jan, as do some of his friends, but doesn't interfere with her sexually, both because he has some inkling of the violence of father's reaction if he was discovered, and that he has other interests with his male friends, like football and videos. Jan responds to Simon warily, unless father is around, when she cries every time father gives attention to Simon. In this shared milieu, Jan knows who she is and how she is seen. This knowledge informs her actions and her expectations of how her environment will react to her.

An interesting point to note is that, in spite of her dependency on her parents, particularly her mother (who does most of the day-to-day providing), Jan has been a separate, choosing entity from birth onwards, with expanding arenas in which she can exercise her choices as her familiarity with the world and her control over her body develop. It is only later, aged six months, that she has been able to move to a position of what Stern calls 'Self with Other,' of 'we' rather than 'I and you,' in this case with her father, maybe with a particular friend at the childminder's. This is in sharp distinction to earlier theorists of child development such as Margaret Mahler, who assumed that the newborn infant was in total symbiosis with mother, and only later achieves separation. The experiments Stern and his team conducted to show the infant's autonomous powers of choice are fascinating and worth reading.

At this time, aged eight months, Jan takes another developmental step. From her developing ability to be intimate, Jan is coming to realize that other people are people like herself.

This is the start of what Stern calls the *intersubjective* domain of self. She is learning to understand how other people get to do what they are doing. Given Jan's experiences, her ability to do this is to some extent limited and skewed. She is more able to step into men's worlds than women's. Jan also has comparatively little ability to understand other children.

What Jan, and her parents as well, find difficult is keeping a simultaneous sense of herself and of other people. Thus, with father, Jan gets his attention by acting in ways which she knows that he will like, without checking with herself whether she wants something different. At root, it is his approval and attention that she likes. With mother, Jan pays attention to her own wants, rather than taking mother's wants into account. This is reinforced by father's pleasure when Jan and her mother get into a conflict.

If we can skip forwards a few years, as Jan gets older, her impairment at this level of relating becomes quite obvious. Her relationship with her parents does not really change. With other children, Jan's difficulties in understanding them is a major limitation, especially when they play children's games or explore their own and each other's bodies in a playful way by play fighting or bathroom trips. The physical game she plays is 'the other woman' in relation to her parents. She masturbates quite often. She either appears older than her age and more at home with adults than other children; or quite babyish with tantrums and petulance.

Jan began to speak at around 15 months. This does not mean that language was not meaningful to her before then. For several months, she had been picking up meanings of simple words and phrases spoken by other people. From her growing identification with other people as well as her innate instincts, she has become aware of her potential to communicate in this way. (We know that both are needed to develop language skills from studies of 'wolf children' who miss out on the possibility of identification with other people who speak to them.) She has needed to develop much more precise motor skills with her mouth, lungs and throat to be able to copy any sound clearly enough to be understood. In fact, I imagine that a simple first sound combination would be a vocalization first through closed mouth ('mm'), then opening her mouth ('aa'). Rather than being the first word babies learn, my guess is that this natural sound 'mama,' or something similar ('baba,' 'dada') would be adopted pretty universally as a name for mother. In any case, when Jan said 'mama,' she caused great excitement in her family, and pleasant attention from her mother that she didn't usually get, so she said it more often.

As Jan's speaking developed, her experience changed in a number of ways. She slowly created a world of words and concepts, parallel to her perceptual world. This world became increasingly sophisticated and differentiated, and also increasingly linked to Jan's perceptual world, so that what Jan saw and heard would be filtered through a screen of language and concepts. One of the concepts would be the concept of Jan herself. This is a kind of *splitting*, where Jan, who was hitherto an 'I,' became also a 'me,' whom she could talk about, and even to. So she would say "Jan wants a biscuit.", or, if she gets hurt, "Poor Jan." This put in place a major aspect of Jan's *personality function*, the 'verbal replica of self' (PHG). What is more, she can make the verbal personality diverge from sense data, in several different ways. She can fantasize, playfully: "Jan is a princess.", or, given her history: "Jan is married to Daddy." She can tell a lie: "Jan didn't break that," and believe it just as much as she believed her play of being a princess.

The other aspect of Jan's verbal functioning was that she could get a much more specific understanding of what people, especially her parents, wanted of her. She could therefore also be more actively 'naughty.' She could say "No," sometimes because she didn't want to do something, sometimes because she wanted to be different, and use her ego function of *alienation* to explore the boundary between herself and other people. Her parents said she was entering the 'terrible twos.'

Jan's father oscillated between finding this funny and charming, and, if he was inconvenienced, being angry and slapping her. Jan learned to gauge this quite well. Her mother was more likely to be angry and slap, but often would feel tired and harassed,

143

and 'try to ignore it,' i.e. cut off. This would get into a downward spiral: Jan would experience rejection, the loss of the boundary she wanted to explore, and escalate her behavior. Mother would withdraw more, Jan would escalate more. Eventually, to Jan's relief, she would get slapped, which was attention, and a boundary of a sort. Sometimes, Jan would be egged on to fight mother by father, who would stand on the sidelines and laugh, and get angry with mother when she got angry with Jan.

Of course, the other change that had been happening was that Jan was by this stage mobile, first crawling and then walking. Her mobility plus her experiments with being different were sometimes quite a strain on her parents. It was much simpler when Jan went to her playgroup. She did her same boundary-testing naughtiness, but was met with much clearer boundaries, so she and the playgroup leader could find a much easier accommodation where, quite literally, they both knew who they were.

There is just one more life stage that I want to talk about: Puberty and teenage years. As Jan got to twelve years old, she started looking to the rest of her family more like a woman than a girl. As you may have gathered, the family was in any case rather confused about the generational boundaries, with Jan being treated more and more as a surrogate wife by her father, and an object of sexual interest by her brother. Thus the fact of her obvious sexual development introduced a number of changes. Father was dimly aware of the incestuous logic of his view of Jan, and, rather than acting on that, withdrew from her physically. Jan's brother started making suggestive remarks to her and trying to get to peep at her in the bathroom or bedroom. Mother felt a whole mixture of feelings. Her own experience of sexuality was not a positive one, and she had several conversations with Jan about 'being careful.' She also, in a very unacknowledged way, saw a useful potential in Jan developing a sexual interest in boys her own age: This would be a separation from her closeness with father, which mother found irksome and sometimes disgusting.

Jan herself felt the separation from father and at the same time felt his sexual interest, and used all her flirtatious skills to try and get closer again. This in turn drove him further away. She then diverted her interest to being flirtatious with boys a couple of years older than herself, subtly encouraged by mother. Her first full sexual encounter was at 14, with a boy of 16, which, given her history, did not feel like a radical departure.

At the same time, Jan was intellectually bright enough to do reasonably well at school, being above the midrange of the class. She learned fairly easily, especially with teachers she liked, and who liked her. Her science was good enough for her eventually to get into further education, then a job in a laboratory.

At age 17, Jan moved out of her parental home to live with her boyfriend, age 25. She would never have considered moving out to live on her own — she did not experience herself as a complete person in her own right.

●

What I am hoping to get across in this fictitious history is that, in Jan's relational development, which is synonymous with the development of her self, we can see the laying down of patterns which are still recognizable with the adult woman who comes for therapy. This is not directly because we are a 'product of our childhood.' The importance of Jan's childhood was that she learned certain patterns of understanding and being in the world, which equate with certain ways of being herself, which she did not at the time have the independence or the perspective to question. Those patterns are literally *familiar*, from the family. She would try to get her needs met in the ways which would be successful in her family.

In Jan's adult world, these patterns would either not work, or only work if she related to people who constellated themselves in the same way as her childhood family did (and this Jan would encourage the people around her to do). The here-and-now habitual action is her limiting of her awareness and contacting in order to avoid the anxiety of the unfamiliar. In some ways there might be some specific consequences, for example rejection, that she is afraid of incurring. However, the central *impasse* is the anxiety connected with a loss of what makes Jan herself, the *death layer* of a landscape without the signposts or landmarks Jan expects. Here there is a death and rebirth to be gone through. No wonder her fantasies include suicide.

Chapter 9

DIALOGUE AND EXPERIMENT

For many people, Gestalt therapy is synonymous with a set of experimental techniques, particularly the 'empty chair' and fantasy dialogues. More recently, there has been a swing away from the use of experiment and towards an emphasis on 'dialogic therapy,' coupled with an interest in the work of Martin Buber and the 'intersubjective' theorists such as Stolorow (Stolorow, Atwood & Brandchaft, 1994).

The question I would like to address here is: What is the meaning and place of dialogue and experiment in Gestalt therapy? I shall also connect this with the question of the meaning and place of self-support, environmental support and confrontation in Gestalt therapy.

What is dialogue?

My contentions here are that there is a particular sense in which Gestalt therapy is dialogic, that this kind of dialogue *includes* experiment, and that in that sense Fritz Perls was often highly dialogic. The dialogue practiced by Buber and Perls emphasizes differentiation and contact rather than empathy and attunement. It was not a soft option. A good example of this approach comes from the Buber scholar (and Buber's friend), Maurice Friedman (1990), of his relationship with a suicidal student:

> At the end of the quarter she said, 'I don't have a paper for you but I'll write you a letter about the paper I will write.' Again I said, 'Fine.' Then she announced to me that she was going to go to Helen Lynd instead of myself for the rest of the year. Once again I said 'Fine, but you still have to write that paper for me.' Then she would come to me and say, 'I'm getting closer to the subway trains. What's more important to you? That paper or my life?' I said, 'You're the one who wants credit. What's more important to you?' I held out . . . I was the one person she kept in touch with after she graduated . . . I could not confirm her life saying, 'Oh well, Margie is in danger and therefore I just have to play it soft.' I mean I had to risk, even, the possibility of her suicide. That's real confirmation.

All Gestalt 'objects' are relational: Self, other, meaning, awareness, all are, to use Carl Hodges' term, *events* at the contact boundary. A therapy based on such a relational outlook cannot fail to be dialogic, i.e. to emphasize that growth occurs in the contact and relationship between the therapist and the client, rather than 'internally' in the client. The contact boundary both joins and separates self and other, organism and environment. The task of the therapist is to act as an 'other' in relation to which the client can explore and develop 'self.' What is 'between' (using Buber's term) is the contact boundary. The contact *is* the differentiation, followed by the meeting, leading to a moment of 'final contact,' where the boundary between contacter and contacted falls and both are open to change.

This to me is precisely analogous to the 'I-Thou moment' of Buber, with the added emphasis that it is not seen as being possible merely with another human being. Buber has sometimes been taken to support the idea that we make our contact with other human beings absolutely central, and correspondingly neglect our non-human environment (something which, with global warming and the destruction of the ozone layer, human beings need like a hole in the head!). One of the nice aspects of PHG is how it places human awareness in the wider context of the natural world. In fact, Buber is not so totally geared to human-to-human contact, and talks about the individual being:

> . . . in *real contact*, in real reciprocity with the world
> in all the points in which the world can meet man.
> I don't say only with man, because sometimes we
> meet the world in other shapes than that of man.
> (Buber in Kirschenbaum & Henderson (eds.),
> 1990)

An important aspect of the Gestalt dialogic approach is that it is primarily *non-verbal*. Perls took from his analysis with Reich the latter's insight that what the client *does* is a far more reliable guide to the process of the client than what he says. Gestalt therapy is not a 'meeting of minds.' In fact, as I have said, PHG understands 'mind' as an *unavoidable illusion* in a complex society where "there exists a chronic low-tension disequilibrium, a continual irk of danger and frustration, interspersed with occasional acute crises, and never fully relaxed" (PHG) which keeps us in a continuous state of 'chronic low grade emergency.'

This emphasis on the non-verbal brings back into the Gestalt dialogic approach the analytic concept of *therapeutic abstinence*. Maintaining the dialogue does not mean that I need to do a lot of speaking, to answer the client's questions, or to say much about myself. I can uphold my side of the dialogue by my attention and interest, the expression in my eyes, or my adjustment of distance between me and the client, rather than by finding a verbal response every time. Harris (1996) has written cogently on the value and power of silence in therapy, and also (personal communication, paraphrasing Laura Perls) that as the therapist's skill level increases, he can "have the knack of doing 'as much as necessary, as little as possible."

Thus for me the keynotes for dialogue in Gestalt therapy are:

Willingness to stay as an other for the client.
Commitment to the client and his growth.
Willingness to share myself with the client, but not to push myself onto him.
Clarity in what I require from the client: Fee, no violence, a willingness to engage with the process with me.
Willingness to try and understand how the client sees the world, without giving up on how I see the world (Buber called this 'inclusion')

A more technical way of saying all these is that I keep myself as much as possible precisely at the contact boundary, neither entering the client's psychological space, nor taking myself away from the client. A good analogy is the 'pushing hands' exercise in Tai Ch'i, maintaining contact, keeping moving so I neither push the other over nor let myself be pushed over.

Dialogue, empathy and attunement

The distinguishing feature of Gestalt dialogue is the emphasis on the 'otherness' of the therapist as a *prerequisite* of the selfhood of the client and the possibility of meeting. In such a dialogic approach, *empathy* is quite a problematic concept. To quote Resnick (1995):

The constant empathic response *á la* Kohut is an attempt to establish and maintain 'attunement' with the client. Functionally, this requires the frequent (if not constant) denial of the *therapist's* phenomenology in favor of the *client's* phenomenology, making any kind of real contact or dialogue completely impossible. (Italics in original)

As Gestaltists, we need to be wary of concepts such as 'empathic attunement,' 'mirroring,' or 'meeting developmental needs': This attunement was lacking in childhood, and therefore the client cannot continue to the next developmental phase until she gets it from the therapist. Rather, we would be thinking more in terms of what Buber called 'inclusion' — the interest and understanding of another person who is other and therefore contactable — and 'confirmation' — valuing who this person is at this moment *and* the person's movement into who she will become. Most of all, to quote Buber (in Kirschenbaum & Henderson (eds.), 1990):

. . . for what I call dialogue, there is essentially necessary the moment of surprise . . . a man can surprise himself. But in a very different manner from how a person can surprise another person.

Our clients come with 'unfinished business' from childhood and elsewhere, and have become adept at finding spurious ways to finish it. The neurotic limits his world to those areas where the painful feelings stay in the background. The borderline clings confluently to someone else or to a drug or sex in an attempt to drown out the pain of making contact or just being seen—and flips into rage and despair when the other person tries to make some distance. The narcissist essentially splits herself in two and primarily relates across the split (retroflection) rather than with the environment.

These are all avoidances of the pain of saying goodbye to the hope of ever getting what I wanted from the person I wanted it from, in the way I wanted it; and of facing the 'surprise' of real dialogue with the other. Marvelously, having allowed myself to grieve, I can find that the world is now big enough to provide the things I now developmentally need: Contact, affirmation, challenge, love, the unpredictable, play, places to withdraw. Now I can get what I need, not as a 'replacement' for what I didn't get as a child, but in contact with the wider, richer world available to me now.

In therapy, the client can get some of this contact from the therapist, not as a prerequisite to healing, but as a *result* of the healing that comes from despairing of and saying goodbye to childhood hopes. This despair is the 'impasse' leading to the implosive 'death layer' of Perls' (1969) five-layer model of neurosis. Before the client says goodbye, the Gestalt therapist interested in real dialogue must avoid playing a replacement parent, thus depriving the client of real contact. The therapist needs sensitivity to the client's need for pacing and grading of her giving up, and this is where contact skills are important. Some clients will not be willing to undertake this work and will leave, and this will sometimes be to do with mistiming of therapist interventions; often it will be an unwillingness to face the pain they begin to feel as being inherent in the work. This is fine, and not necessarily a therapist blunder.

The opposite view is presented by Tobin (1982):

> An example of (being more confrontative than the patient could tolerate) and its results is a patient who left therapy after only one session and returned for group three years later. I said to this man, 'I don't feel any contact with you' in our first session. I said this in what I thought was a kindly voice and for the purpose of letting him know that

I thought an important feature of his was his inability to make real contact with others and that this would be something we would work on. Three years later, when he returned in great despair as a last resort to try group therapy with me, he told me that he knew that what I had said three years earlier was true, but that he had felt so hurt by my comment that he didn't think he could work with someone who was so insensitive to him.

My question is, why is this an 'error'? Interestingly, I don't think Buber would have seen it as an error at all! Tobin's assumption is that his comment 'hurt' the client. Rather, my assumption is that the client's acknowledgment of the validity of this comment opened the door for him to experience the hurt and shame he brought with him. At that stage he made the choice to leave therapy rather than stay with a therapist who would not be confluent with his wish to avoid the hurt. However, he remembered him! He returned to Tobin after three years 'in despair' ready to work. Fine: That one session gave him a link to someone he knew told the truth, and was willing to make contact. His process continued, he reached his point of despair, and returned to Tobin. And for this he only paid for one session! Would that man's life have been better if he'd stayed with a therapist who 'empathically attuned' with him for three years instead? We do not know. My guess would be the opposite of Tobin's.

Support and confrontation

Perls defined the goal of Gestalt therapy as a movement from manipulating the environment for support to self-support. This has sometimes been taken to mean that Perls' view of maturity was to do everything for ourselves, and not to get support from the environment. I have often heard it stated that Perls identified too much with the individualistic 'self-support' pole, and ignored the opposite pole of environmental support. This is sometimes a valid criticism. But let us look at Perls (1973):

> The individual's chance of physical survival is almost nil if he is left entirely to himself. Man needs others to survive physically. His psychological and emotional survival chances are even lower if he is left alone ... Man's sense of relatedness to the group is as natural to him as his sense of relatedness to any one of his physiological survival impulses. (p. 25)

How does this fit with an emphasis on 'self-support'? Look at the next sentence:

> The gestalt approach, which *considers the individual as a function of the organism/environment field,* and which considers his behavior as reflecting his relatedness within that field, gives coherence to this conception of man as both an individual and as a social creature.

The 'self' in 'self-support' is PHG's self, not Descartes' ghost in the machine! This self comes as much from environment as from the organism. It is what chaos theory calls 'emergent': Self emerges from the interaction rather than from the participants in the interaction. Self then acts on both sides of the contact boundary to support its selfhood. This is feedback or homoeostasis. The organism will be opened to — and move towards — what is novel and/or nourishing in the environment and closed to — and move away from — what is toxic; the environment will be altered (aggressed upon) to provide food, human contact, creativity and pleasure in various forms. Part of the balance will be that organism and environment need to be in good contact. It is not just that part of self-support is getting support from the environment; rather,

Peter-'self,' arising on the contact boundary, is a function of Peter-environment as much as of Peter-organism. For example, a client making eye-contact with me, seeing my willingness to be present with her, and taking support from that *is* (contact-based) self-support.

If I manipulate the environment for support, on the other hand, I will be parceling up I/organism and dumping it onto the environment, saying "Look after this." My actions will not be based on my wants, needs and interests in contact with the environment, but on what will get a response from that environment that feels good to me. These interactions do not arise from contact with the environment, but from manipulation. Paradoxically, such interactions are much more 'selfish' than the contactful interactions arising from self-support.

Extreme versions of this loss of self-support are 'nervous breakdowns,' where people in effect deny their own responsibility for their behavior, and even for their survival. The person is not contactable, while at the same time powerfully manipulating those around him. For example, a client not looking at me, but wanting me to say words to the effect of "I support you" (whatever that means!) to make himself feel better is both a manipulation of me, and also of himself. Not only might I be lying: I *would* be lying, since I would be uttering an entirely vacuous phrase as if it were meaningful. Perls was not pathologizing support from the environment, but the break in the contacting process that turns this into manipulation.

Full contact is lost by the accretion of 'unfinished business,' which pushes for attention and takes energy from the present contacting. The 'autonomous criterion' points to where this good contact has been lost, by noticing where the gestalts formed lack color, grace, coherence and 'good form.' Restoration of contact comes through the therapist's frustration of, and bringing to awareness of, the client's unaware neurotic (unchoiceful) strategies for avoiding contact, her attempts to manipulate the world into supporting a familiar pattern (even where the client knows that pattern does not serve her well).

I assume (like Perls) that what clients want from me when they come into therapy will usually not be helpful for them — if they could ask so easily, they wouldn't have needed to ask for it from a therapist! — and I need, especially at the start of therapy, not to be confluent with what they overtly want. I might offer contact in a different way, or ask them what would happen if I did as they asked, or get them to play the therapist and reply, or tell them I want to get to know them better and what is it like to be here with me now? Later, when they are more in contact with their here-and-now wants, needs and interests, I am much more willing to give them what they want.

If this seems very loaded onto the pole of frustration, I want to emphasize that the aim is to restore contact, and for this I need to be available as fully as possible for contact. I need to be clear (with them and in myself) that I am not frustrating out of malice, or some sadistic wish to hurt the client, but out of interest and respect for the whole of the client, not just the neurotic demands. I would link this with Wheeler's (1991) discussion of the need for the therapist not to be 'figure-bound'; I would consider it more accurate to say that I must ensure that my figure is not confluent with the client's figure.

The significance of this for a Gestalt dialogic approach is that I am present in the therapy as another real person, and not as a 'supporter' or a 'helper,' nor in confluence with the client's expectations. Sometimes I might support or help, sometimes I will challenge or frustrate, but these will flow out of our contact, from what is genuine, rather than to manipulate the client into feeling better, or to help me feel more altruistic. In terms of ego functions, my contact with the client will sometimes emphasize alienation or difference, and sometimes will emphasize identification or similarity. However, the theory of selfhood on which Gestalt therapy is based says that my starting point must be difference (as much as can be tolerated) and willingness to make contact from that difference, otherwise the contacting process cannot begin.

Empowerment

The most chilling moment in Molly Dineen's brilliant BBC2 series on the financial crisis of the London Zoo came when she was interviewing one of the directors. He was explaining the necessity for *empowerment* of the staff. 'Once you've given them empowerment,' he said, 'you've got them in the grinder.'" (Ward, 1993)

Underlying the debate around support and confrontation is often the question of the 'empowerment' of clients. Given a client who, from fear, holds back from taking her power in the environment, what would be the best response from the therapist? It is clear that it would feel most comfortable for the client if the therapist holds back on his power, and emphasizes his willingness to accept what the client chooses. Unfortunately, from my perspective the effect of this is paradoxical: By implication, if I do this I am saying to the client that I have the ability to make her feel more 'empowered.' This makes me the powerful one! Thus the more I work to empower a client, the more I disempower her.

My basic assumption is that the only thing I can do is to be present as powerfully as I can be without the client either walking out or moving into uncontactful terror; the client can then choose whether to risk meeting me powerfully or not. I need to ensure that my power is not based on a wish to control my client nor in playing out some 'unfinished business' of my own. Thus a prerequisite for my being available for such a powerful and healing meeting is that I remain in good contact with myself and also using my contact functions (seeing, hearing) accurately with my client.

Peter: I just saw you stop breathing, and your eyes defocused. What's happened?

Jan: I suddenly felt scared and ashamed. I thought that you could see right through me.

P: Uh-huh . . . It's important that you don't enter this fear and shame while out of contact, even though that seems like the thing to do. If you need to take a break or walk around for a time, let me know. Otherwise, I suggest you keep glancing at me, to see my real reaction to you rather than the one you fear.

(My experience is that, in acknowledging a client's fear and/or shame without trying to make it more comfortable, I facilitate her working through these feelings in contact with the reality of myself rather than the projections which are much more powerful if I show my power less:)

J: I'm scared that you think I shouldn't be saying these things.

P: Is your experience of me that I would hold back from saying this if I felt it?

J: (Considers, then laughs) No, I think you'd tell me.

P: I am not holding out on you!

Experiment

This brings us on to the role of the experiment in Gestalt therapy, and its relation to the dialogue. Some writers on dialogic Gestalt therapy (e.g. Jacobs, Hycner) downgrade experiments, on the basis that the therapist giving the client an experiment to do removes the horizontal relationship between therapist and client. The therapist becomes the expert, the client becomes the one who obeys and takes the prescription. This is an argument that must be taken seriously. *Every* intervention that I make as a therapist affects my relationship to the client, because every intervention involves a configuration of our field, and is an invitation to the client to act in a complementary way.

The concept that seems most relevant to me here is the **balance of expertise**. This is a boundary issue. The client's sphere of expertise is to be himself; to choose his own present and future; to find his best creative adjustment to the environment unless he has disrupted the process out of anxiety; and to show these areas to the therapist in the therapy relationship. The therapist's area of expertise is on a different level entirely: To offer and maintain a therapeutically bounded relationship; to be able to use her senses (seeing, hearing, etc.) acutely and accurately; to be in good contact with her own experience, especially in response to the client; and the creativity to target an experiment to the stuck areas, combined with the creativity to know when it is or is not appropriate to suggest an experiment.

Thus there is no inherent problem for me as a therapist showing my expertise: After all, the client is paying me for doing this! However, part of the expertise is knowing that some clients will turn any suggestion of mine into a demand, and abase themselves before my power; other clients will, equally unchoicefully, refuse any suggestion of mine. I would not suggest any experiments to clients who do this. Some kinds of experiment are still possibly in order: With a client who raises me up, I could sit lower, or even prostrate myself in front of her. The experiment then involves *me* doing something, rather than suggesting that the client does something. The client can, if she wishes, notice how she responds. It is useful to be aware of these two categories of experiments: Where I suggest that the client does something, and where I do something unexpected but relevant, and we both see what happens.

The experiment in Gestalt therapy fulfills a particular function. It is not, in my opinion, a form of behavior modification — although, unfortunately, Zinker (1977 & 1994) does describe it in this way. I connect the Gestalt experiment with the concept of the *safe emergency* and the move in Perls' 'five layer' model of neurosis from the 'role-playing layer' to the 'impasse' (Perls, 1969 for all these concepts). That is, the client is offered an opportunity to explore the limits they impose on their acting and relating; and via this to open the prospect of reintegrating alienated possibilities, while accessing their anxieties round doing so.

There are essentially three experimental methods in Gestalt therapy: *Enactment with awareness* (slowing down), *exaggeration* and *reversal*. I shall describe these in turn.

Enactment with awareness

C: I find it very difficult to look at you.

T: Would you be willing to look away, then move your eyes slowly towards me and describe what you notice as you do that: bodily sensations, what you see, thoughts, fantasies?

C: OK. I'm moving my eyes towards you . . . my stomach feels tense . . . I feel frightened . . . I am imagining you looking at me with cold, angry eyes, disapproving.

T: As your eyes, what might you be saying to me?

C: I don't want to see your anger, so I keep away from you. That's what I used to do with my father!

In this experiment, something the client habitually does is enacted in a new frame: An experiment, freely chosen, done slowly with awareness. This new frame allows the fantasy of cold, angry eyes to emerge in awareness. My fantasy is then of a dialogue of eyes, and I suggest speaking as the eyes. This allows for the fantasy to be connected to a memory, in this case. Notice though that I am not 'going for' a fantasy, or a memory, or anything in particular. What emerges is what emerges. Most of the experiments that I do are of this kind. For me the key is *slowing down*. Even a client's fantasy of killing me or hitting her head against a wall becomes enactable if done slowly and with awareness.

Exaggeration

T: You could experiment with saying to your father, "I will not stay with your anger."

C: I find that scary — I could never say that to him openly. I'll give it a try though . . . I will not stay with your anger (small jerk of right hand and arm).

T: Will you repeat that, and exaggerate the arm movement?

C: I will not stay with your anger (hitting the settee she's sitting on).

T: Again.

C: (Angry voice) I will not stay with your anger (hitting settee) . . . and I'm angry too now.

The point of the exaggeration — of definiteness ("I don't want to . . . " to "I will not . . . ") and of physical movement — is that parts of the action have been minimized. The aim is not to exaggerate it beyond its rightful place, but to allow it its rightful place, to experiment with going beyond the habitual limitations. Thus I might encourage someone who is breathing shallowly to breathe more deeply, but not to breathe beyond a natural level of breathing (although it might seem unnatural to the client). My aim is not the 'discharge' of emotion, merely the contactful expression of what is there. It is easy to get carried away by the drama of high emotion. For me, whatever drama there is in Gestalt therapy must be a *real* drama, rather than a poor melodrama of beating a moustache-twirling villain to death in order to release the maiden in distress.

161

Reversal

T: Now could you be father's eyes and reply: I am cold and angry
. . .

C: I am cold and angry, you are an ungrateful girl and I'm glad you stay away from me. I'm glad I sent you away to school.

T: Switch back, and speak to father in the same way, cold and angry.

C: I am also glad that I went away from you. I had so much love to give you and you pushed me away. Every time I tried to come close I got hurt. You do not deserve my love . . . and yet I still do love you and miss you.

This reversal is the classic Gestalt 'empty chair' (whether or not the client actually moves). This method is very easy to misunderstand, and to treat as a behavioral learning in assertiveness, finding new ways of relating to father. For me, this is not the point. The 'father' here is not really father, it is a disowned pole of the client, disowned because she did not like it when father acted like that (see also my discussion of introjection). However, in disowning that polarity she made it very problematic to relate to people who act in that way. She either clings or hides. She does not allow herself the separated contact, tinged with anger, that might be the only contact available, though other contact can grow from it, as it does at the end of this vignette. Nor does she allow herself to understand on a human level the human frailty from which he acts as he does, so that she either must go on blaming him, or, more likely, blaming herself.

The aim of using the empty chair is to facilitate *integration* of the different aspects through the dialogue, to allow an arena where the different state-dependent systems can coexist, and to focus on the 'ring-fencing' process. Now this is clear where the 'people' on the chairs are obviously aspects of one person. Confusion about the technique can set in where there appears to be other people on the cushions with which the client is dialoguing. For example, the client could be talking to mother, or boss, or landlord. Very quickly the technique becomes a behavioral one of practicing new ways of dealing with a difficult situation. Sometimes people can even find this useful. It is not, however, the Gestalt meaning of the technique. For Gestalt, the people and situations we find problematic are primarily ones where we are faced with situations which our self-limited character cannot easily deal with, because we have excluded from our range the relational possibilities of the people we now have to deal with.

Let us pause a moment on this point, for there is an immediate objection here. What about someone in a state of poverty or hunger, where things are difficult for fully external reasons? The distinction I want to make here is between *problematic* situations and *painful* ones. Life sometimes offers only a limited choice between painful possibilities. If I accept the pain inherent in a period in my life, my life will be painful but not overwhelmingly problematic. Therapy will not make that pain any less, except maybe that I will benefit by not trying desperately to change the inevitable. If I do not accept the pain, then I will find life problematic as well as painful. In exploring my non-acceptance, I can maybe get to a point where I allow myself to accept my situation, resolving the problem that way. I may also choose to deny myself acceptance, preferring to continue fighting against, say, the injustice of my situation even though I have little hope of significantly changing it. So long as I am aware of the reality of my environmental situation, and honest with myself about the choices I am making, my situation, while remaining painful, ceases to be problematic. I am of course aware that the majority of people who are living in poverty or hunger can not avail themselves of psychotherapy, and would not consider it their priority anyway: That also is part of reality.

So, back to the 'empty chair.' I hope it is clear from what I have said above that, even where the 'occupant' of one of the chairs is an identifiable person in the client's life, the only person who the client can play is himself. The person the client is encountering is an excluded relational possibility for him. The most significant chair in this dialogue is not the one representing the client as he knows himself, but the one representing the other. Unfortunately, this is the one which the client often wants to tell to go away, or kill, and it is tempting as a therapist to confluently go along with this. Paradoxically, if we instead value all aspects of the client, as the integration happens the ring-fenced part-self does die, as does the complementary part-self outside the fence. What remains is a wider self choicefully incorporating the possibilities of both of the previous part-selves. Conversely, the part-self that is 'killed' or rejected cannot be integrated, and remains a powerful and covert influence on our behavior.

I want to look at one particular situation which at first glance seems different to the way in which I am discussing empty chair work: Saying "goodbye" to someone who has died. This is one of the most beautiful uses of this technique, often leading to profound changes for people. The person on the empty chair is the person who has died. This person is 'resurrected' to dialogue with the client.

Although it looks as if this is a clear case in which the important role is the client saying their goodbye, in fact the same considerations apply: There is some aspect of the dead person's remembered way of being with which the client has 'unfinished business,' so they are not willing to let them pass away. It may be that they just need extra time and support to come to terms with the world without a loved one. Or it may be that they are still looking to a parent for love or support that has not been forthcoming, or for permission to act in a new way. They may bind themselves to the other person by ropes of hate, and this would be paralleled by the kind of ring-fencing which I described above. In the end, it is when they can assimilate all aspects of the dead person's way of being within themselves that they can say goodbye to them! This is a familiar kind of paradox within Gestalt.

In any event, there is a need for something from their introject of the dead person before the living person can let him or her go. This could be just being willing to listen; or being willing to accept the other person; or giving a clear message that they will *never* accept the other person whatever hoops they jump through, so that the latter can say goodbye to and mourn not only the person who has died, but also their hopes that things could be different if they were better or cleverer or other than they are. As the character played by John Cleese says in the film *Clockwise*, "I can stand the despair, it's the hope . . . "

The 'empty chair' is not the only form of reversal experiment: Other possible forms are: to reverse posture (e.g. sitting closed to sitting open); to reverse voice tone (e.g. loud to soft); to reverse physical distance (e.g. standing distant to standing close); to reverse characteristic (e.g. someone who characteristically gives can experiment with taking).

Experiment and creativity

If the experiment is going to be part of a lively relationship with the client, in which the client is invited to move beyond her habitual limitations, I as therapist must be willing to make my part of the experimental process a creative one, emerging from my contact with the client rather than from a set of standardized experiments, known to produce a standard reaction. Remember, I am facilitating the client to be *unpredictable* — even to me.

Thus I am using the term 'experiment' in its real scientific sense of something new allowing for different outcomes than in the 'school laboratory' sense of doing something that has been done many times before, knowing that there will be a standard outcome unless my technique is faulty. Thus I am creating an experiment that encapsulates my good understanding of where the client is, and where our relationship is. Otherwise, we 'go through the motions' with each other. This is an example of the dual nature of 'homoeostasis': To maintain our relationship as a contactful and nourishing one, the therapist (and hopefully eventually the client) needs to be creatively open to the client's changing phenomenology.

Dialogue and experiment

When the Gestalt experiment is viewed in this way, it becomes part of my dialogic relationship with the client, giving him the opportunity to contact me and the rest of his environment in different ways. Part of the dialogic (non-confluent) aspect of this is the fact that we are both coming from our own area of therapeutic expertise, and that I will be aware that there are circumstances when I would not be willing to suggest anything:

T: I see a difficulty. I get the sense that you are waiting for me to give you something to do. My fantasy is that you would then do it for me, rather than checking out with yourself your willingness to do it, or its rightness for you at this moment. Since the aim of this therapy is finding yourself, that would be self-defeating. I'm not sure how we can resolve this.

Here, staying with this dilemma *is* the impasse. The only way we can resolve it (or any therapeutic impasse) is if the client acts authentically from her needs and wants. Any Gestalt experiment must make figural the impasse inherent in our dialogue, and will then act in the service of the dialogue rather than detracting from it.

To recap, Gestalt therapy is inherently dialogic because all its concepts are relational, and selfhood itself emerges from relationship. Dialogic Gestalt therapy emphasises the exploration of contact, which is not necessarily verbal. In this exploration, therapist responses will sometimes be experienced as supportive and affirming, sometimes as frustrating or confrontative, and hopefully often as both. In their emergence from the relationship between therapist and client, experiments form part of the dialogue, and it is incumbent on the therapist to monitor the relational meaning of proposing a particular experiment at a particular moment in the therapy.

The aim of the experiment is to invite the client beyond a habitual way of being into an exploration of new possibilities for being in the world. Then, even if the client decides to move back into habitual functioning, that will be phenomenologically different, because it will be a choice, made in awareness, rather than compliance with a decision made in different circumstances, often many years before.

Chapter 10

INDIVIDUAL AND GROUP THERAPY

In this chapter, I shall write about a new field-based paradigm for groups and groupwork developed by myself and John Bernard Harris, and discuss the respective advantages of individual and group Gestalt therapy. I shall also look at individual therapy *as* a group therapy, taking into account the living environment of the individual client.

Fundamental to my discussion here is my wish to take a consistent *field* approach to Gestalt therapy, and my view that we have been ill-served by adopting uncritically a more systems-based theory of both individual and group process. This has been borne out by our experience of the effectiveness of a Gestalt groupwork based on this field approach. If Gestalt therapy is an exploration of the client's process of self-actualisation in relation to her environment, then there is a good case for making that environment as experientially rich as possible, and also as experientially close to the client's everyday environment as is therapeutically practical. Group therapy thus has potential advantages over individual therapy, depending on whether the way of running the group is consistent with the field outlook. However, in our individualistic times, many Gestaltists have abandoned group therapy altogether, or limited it to training situations. I shall say more about the practice of groupwork later. First I shall introduce my approach to groupwork theory.

A NEW PARADIGM FOR GROUP WORK THEORY

Over the period of my interest in groups and groupwork, I have talked to and learned from a number of skilled group theorists from a variety of different theoretical backgrounds. Often we have ended up talking at cross purposes in a rather confusing way.

What is becoming clearer to me (and to my co-therapist John Bernard Harris) is that behind these different approaches lies something more basic: A different understanding of what a group is, and what it means to be 'in a group.' I believe we are working in two different *paradigms* in the sense of Kuhn (1970). This means not only that our assumptions are different, but that the meaningful questions are different, and words which we both use ('group,' 'membership,' 'in,' 'out,' 'group process') mean different things.

The assumptions that I understand to be behind the usual paradigm of groups are:

A group is constituted by being together physically.

A group becomes more of a group when people so arrange themselves that everyone can witness any interaction (so in a circle or concentric circles with larger groups).

A group becomes more of a group when people have a 'sense of group.'

A group becomes more of a group when people acknowledge each other's co-membership.

The 'basic assumptions' of a group are absolute points of study, rather than dependent on the character/topology of the group.

So, meaningful questions within this paradigm are: 'Who is in/out?,' 'how to structure the group in order to maximize sense of group?' 'when does a collection of people become a group or stop being a group?'

This paradigm underlies most thinking about groups, from many perspectives: Group analytic, social psychological/T-group, Gestalt and other therapeutic groupwork methods.

A DIFFERENT PARADIGM

I have been becoming more aware of the assumptions behind the way that I understand groups, and that these form the basis for a different paradigm based on *communication*. In this paradigm, group process happens between *any* collection of people who are aware of the *possibility* of intercommunication. Thus any such collection is for me a group.

Whether or not people in the group communicate, who regards themselves as insiders and who as outsiders, and how 'insiders' and 'outsiders' interrelate are all now *part* of the group process.

Whatever happens or doesn't happen in the group is to be understood in relation to the group processes. Its meaning is *field-dependent* rather than absolute.

Groups start having a distinctive process within one minute of their first formation, although this gets elaborated and changed through the life of the group. Groups are very 'sensitively dependent on initial conditions' (Gleick, 1987): The communication possibilities that define them, the geographical space(s) they occupy, how much they are also defined by task, by being called together, by their self-definition as a group, their mythology, who they perceive as leader or led, the state of mind of their members, the history of contributory subgroups, the cultural environment.

Groups so defined in a sense never end, and in another sense are always ending. There will, however, be significant endpoints when members leave or join (however that is defined by the group), or when the group is acknowledged by its members to have ended.

What is the advantage of this much wider definition of groups? The more usual paradigm works well (within limits I discuss below), if we are studying small groups with a specific task or purpose, and an agreed start or finish. The wider definition can produce uninteresting groups, e.g. large, loosely-connected collections of people where all communication is potential. However, a large number of the real-world groupings we are involved with and in move between these extremes. To demonstrate this by a fairly extreme example, consider the people listed in the Manchester telephone directory. This is a group on my definition, but is usually an uninteresting one. However, if telephone charges are suddenly increased, this group's processes could become quite interesting: Which subgroups protest, which change to another telephone provider, who phones whom less, etc.

To take a less strained example, we could look at a small therapy group, and see questions that are approached much more easily from this new paradigm. What is the process of therapy groups between meetings? What are the processes when people arrive for a therapy group? What changes occur between people arriving, maybe getting a drink and assembling, and what processes occur at the time-boundary between this and the group formally 'starting'? Similarly, what happens when a group session 'finishes,' both in the therapy room and when they leave? For me, this is all part of the group process — and, in terms of 'transfer of learning,' is vital to observe.

Or, to take another example, can we talk about the group process of a large industrial concern? Here part of the group process is that (i) everybody does not meet together, (ii) the group is primarily task-oriented, and different parts of the group would probably see their task differently, (iii) the group is formally hierarchical, and probably has many hidden and powerful subgroupings within it, (iv) the membership will be constantly changing, (v) the process of the group will be affected in roughly equal measure by individuals (especially in management, but also in the unions and the research department), by subgroups (departments which have their own processes which might enhance or conflict with larger processes) and by environmental factors (the state of the economy, competitors, sales of their products, cost of their raw materials).

Or take the group consisting of the population of the United Kingdom. We cannot meet together. The gestalt of the group is primarily based on subgroupings: Government, pressure groups, the media, the education system, ethnic and religious groupings, the police and the legal system. Yet it is interesting to chart the processes in this group.

Notice that, on this paradigm, a person is simultaneously a member of a vast number of different groups. They can be seen as members of groups with which they might not wish to be associated. In many cases, people's wish or expectation not to be associated would be a vital part of the definition of the group, whether it is an exclusive club or a confrontational political grouping. That wish not to be associated would be part of the process of those groups. We could put all this into a different language: That of the self. We could say that the group actualizes its group-self in relation to what is alienated as 'other' or outside the group, and what is identified as being inside the group. The boundary of the group is then a continuous creation of identification and alienation, rather than a fixed 'skin.'

APPLICATIONS TO LARGE GROUP METHODOLOGY

The primary patterns of the two paradigms are different. The 'picture' of the first paradigm is a circle (the normal configuration of a small therapy group, or friends sitting round a table). The 'picture' of the second (which I am putting forward) is the 'Street.' In this way of working (introduced by Steve Potter, and taken up in Britain by the Group Relations Training Association) a time and a physical space (maybe more than one room) are set out for a contracted purpose. Within this time and space, people can meet together or not, move or not, join or leave groups (or listen in). A circle is one possible configuration, but so is total non-contact and much in-between.

In the circle, the essence of 'groupness' is seen as the meeting together, the transparency (people talk so everyone can hear), the possibility of everyone speaking (the circle is an egalitarian structure). What is given up to achieve this is movement (although movement can be introduced as a *group exercise*, after which people return to the circle). From this perspective, what is given up by the 'Street' is the transparency, intimacy and sense of wholeness of a group that meets together in one place, generally with just one person talking (to the whole group) at one time.

In the 'Street,' the essence of 'groupness' is in the configuration, the potential for contact, communication and movement, and the process by which this potential is achieved or not achieved. What is given up to achieve this is the concreteness of the circle, any absolute ideas of "this is how a good group functions." From this perspective, what is given up by the circle is movement, generalizability to real-world groups, and, particularly importantly from a Gestalt perspective, the phenomenological approach. In inhibiting the configuration of a group, its possibilities for movement, and the questions that can be posed, become limited and changed. This is true even of a small therapy group (where group members' energy often seems to drain out through their seats), and is vastly more true of large groups.

Maybe a good analogy would be the different approaches of Alexander Technique and Feldenkrais Method. Both work with posture, balance, optimal movement, but in two very different

174

ways. Alexander Technique has a picture of how we should stand, move, sit, and the teacher teaches us these ways. It is concrete and easy to understand. However, to me, people who have done Alexander Technique often look somewhat like robots, as they continuously check their posture. They have learnt a useful introject, and a kind of egotism. More seriously, Alexander Technique presupposes a certain kind of textbook body. Real people, however, have disabilities, have one leg shorter than the other, or tense parts of their musculature due to various physical or psychological processes. Alexander Technique does not account so well for these people. Feldenkrais does not have an image of what postures are best for people, but rather an assumption that by moving with awareness of the muscular and mechanical processes by which we move, we can orient ourselves to our individual best accommodation with gravity and the possibilities of our own bodies. It will come as no surprise to you to discover that I would see Feldenkrais Method as far more in tune with Gestalt theory than Alexander Technique.

Boundaries

Another question which would be answered differently by the two approaches to group discussed here is: What is the nature of the group boundary?

In the 'Circle' group, the boundary that is of primary (or even of sole) importance is the boundary between inside and outside. This boundary is fairly tightly drawn, at least with respect to time and space, and often (especially with smaller groups) quite rigid with respect to membership and seating arrangements. Important considerations are *safety* and *trust*, which are presupposed to depend on these boundaries, and others such as confidentiality, being firmly in place.

In a therapy group based on the 'street,' the boundary of primary interest might be the boundary between inside and outside; it might also be internal boundaries between subgroups in the group, between therapist/facilitator and clients, between the group in session and the group out of session or in different contexts. Rather than an emphasis on safety and trust, the questions are: What am I prepared to do here? What would I need to establish in order to do more? What (if anything) are the real dangers here? What preconceptions do I bring to the situation which frighten me even when I'm safe? In some circumstances, this might mean closing the external boundary, or agreeing on some contract on confidentiality. In others, none of this might be needed.

One actual danger specific to closed groups with a firm external boundary is that this (usually artificial) boundary becomes a projection object for fears of dissolution, of meaninglessness, of aloneness or *anomie*. I remember the image used in one group situation of being adrift on an open sea. I commented that after a certain time, people adrift would end up eating each other! This is enhanced if there is an emphasis on safety, in a similar reaction to if I am flying in an aeroplane in level flight, and the pilot announces suddenly, "There is no cause for alarm." The phrase "establish safety" is taken as an 'implied directive' in the sense of Erickson (1980) to expect danger.

INDIVIDUAL OR GROUP THERAPY?

I have spent some time thinking about the question of when individual or group psychotherapy is more appropriate for a person. I work as an individual and group therapist, and also train and supervise therapists, so the issue often comes up.

First of all, I want to say that from my Gestalt perspective, I believe that ongoing group therapy has a greater potential than individual therapy. My reasons for believing this are based on the Gestalt conception of what therapy is: A mutual exploration of the client's being-in-the-world, and in particular how the client makes contact or avoids contact, and what the client allows himself to become aware of, and what awarenesses he blocks. The client can then use the therapy situation to experiment with new ways of contacting and new areas of awareness. Gestalt is therefore one of the therapies which is less geared to 'fixing' a particular problem, and more towards exploring and allowing change in the relationship to the world in which the problem arises.

So, from this perspective, the group can act as a laboratory, with a wide range of different people, with different perspectives, ways of handling the world, and ways of orienting themselves in the world. In this laboratory, clients can be both supported and challenged, and will show in their relationships within the group how they both act in the world and limit their action in the world.

A group also avoids one of the difficulties of individual therapy, where the client assumes that, if the therapist is saying supportive things, it is not a spontaneous response, but a technique, and only said because they are paying. I find that feedback from other group members is often easier for the client to believe immediately than feedback from the therapist. The group in some way acts as a representation of the world, a panel of peers, with all its judgements, and all its possibilities for comfortable and uncomfortable relating.

Groups are also cheaper than individual private therapy!

I also want to acknowledge that, in some ways rightly, groups have got a bad name. There are some ways in which groups can be profoundly destructive, or not very useful. There were in the past and still are group therapists who use the group to attack individual members who challenge them, so that clients get all their expectations of punishment fulfilled. There must be a good balance of support and challenge in any therapy, so that (for example) if some group members are angry with another member, it is my responsibility as therapist to make sure that the member receiving the anger has sufficient support from me or other members, and to explore with the angry group members what their contribution is to their perception of the object of their anger.

Another problem that can arise in groups is where the therapist sees the group itself as her only client. I believe that in a therapy group, as opposed to a T-group or an Encounter Group for example, each group member is also individually a client of the therapist, and the therapist needs to give time to think about and relate to the therapeutic needs of each person in the group, as well as the needs of the group as a whole.

Another issue that I want to raise here about groups is again the balance between support and challenge. Nobody learns anything (except to hide more effectively and unnoticeably) from being terrified and unsupported. In groups where the climate is one of continuous challenge of members' defenses, without the support of acknowledging their fears and the needs for them to go at their own pace, people often learn to smarten up their coping veneer, while pushing their fears well out of sight.

Conversely, in groups where everybody loves everybody else and everybody gives lots of support, the group becomes a kind of 'charmed circle' where people come in from a 'nasty real world' to be accepted. Of course, their sense of acceptance vanishes the moment they step out of the group room. Of course also this kind of culture where no-one can show their own 'nasty' side means that all the contact is rather artificial. There is only one thing that can develop from this: Confluence and dependency on the group and on the therapist as a refuge from the world. In between these two lies a healing place, where real people, with likes, dislikes and judgements, can find new ways of making contact with each other, ways that can be transferred to an outside world that is not perceived as so different.

Why should anyone go into individual therapy or not go into a group? There are many reasons. The first and most important is that they might want to! Their fear of the group situation might be too great. They might have things to say that they would feel too ashamed to say in front of a group. They might have had bad experiences in groups in the past. They might want time all to themselves in a life where they are fulfilling the requirements of other people a lot of the time. All these are fine reasons for going into individual therapy. None of the advantages I have talked about for groups are insuperable obstacles for individual therapy work.

Some people might have the need for more one-to-one time with the therapist than the therapist is able or willing to give in a group. Some people need to work very slowly, saying very little for a long time. This can often be done better in individual therapy than in a group.

Some people would not fit well into a group. They might put other clients at risk, either of violence or of mind-games that they play, or of sexual acting-out with vulnerable group members. (I have a rule of no sexual relationships between group members: Transference issues cloud such relationships in very similar ways to those well-documented about sexual relationships with therapists). The therapist does have a protective function towards group members, including if necessary protection from other actual or potential group members. Some problematic ways of acting might also make it unsafe for a therapist to take the potential client on individually, some would not.

Some people do best with a mix of individual and group therapy. There are potential problems with this. Clients who come to a group and also see the therapist individually can split themselves between the two, so that in the group they show one aspect of themselves, and show the other aspect to the therapist individually. A culture can build up of group members vying to see the therapist individually, and it can get to the stage where very little useful work is done in the group. However, if the therapist and the client are both aware of these pitfalls, they can in themselves be fruitful areas of exploration: What would be the fear connected with showing this aspect in the group? What is the significance of this split in terms of relating to groups in the client's non-therapy world? How can the client work round to showing their other side in the group? What is the group avoiding by exporting much of its energy to individual sessions?

THE PRACTICE OF GESTALT THERAPY IN A GROUP

What happens in a Gestalt group? It is difficult to make any kind of list, since an important part of the character of such groups is that (within certain safety and ethical boundaries) *anything* can happen. The object, as with individual therapy, is to explore the group members' patterns of contact-making and avoidance, areas of choicefulness and non-choicefulness, awareness and blind-spots.

The three styles of work which I find myself moving between in a group are:

1. *Exploring the interactions between group members*
How does Alan respond to Jane's presence in the group, and *vice versa*? Are they drawn to each other, or do they find themselves in confrontations with each other, or do they find themselves uninterested in each other? What part does each of them play in the interaction, and what is it of themselves that they project onto the other? It is important that we are not just operating an 'encounter group': Perls commented that usually, in such groups, people encounter mainly their own projections, which they then get angry with in the guise of encountering the other person. Thus my rule of thumb in group, as in individual, therapy is to **slow down** the process, for each person to take responsibility for their own actions and motivations. Appropriate questions might be: "What is your interest in pursuing this now?," and "What are you wanting from your angry interchange with Alan?".

Other possibilities for interactive exploration are to invite a group member to play the other group member, and experiment with owning projections, or even for two group members to continue an encounter, both playing the other one. Other group members, and the therapist can give their feedback on the encounter. We need to bear in mind that the aim is to explore each group member's process of self-actualization in the therapy situation.

Example:

Alan: (To Jane) When you speak, I feel myself getting angry. You look needy, yet you never say what you want.

Peter: What do *you* want from Jane, Alan? I understand your statement, and it seems to me there is something extra in your anger.

Alan: (Thinks for a moment) I feel I should help you when you look needy, and then, when I don't know what you want of me, I imagine you being angry with me for not giving you what you want. Then I get angry back.

Peter: What is your experience? Is there any grain of truth in what Alan is imagining?

Jane: Yes, when I get wrapped up in myself, I want someone to notice and get me out.

We could then go on to explore Alan's urge to make it 'all right' for Jane; how it would be (for both) for Alan to say "I don't know how to help you"; how Jane's actions might be a 'gimmick' for getting noticed by withdrawing loudly.

2. A group member working with the therapist
This was the style of group working favored by Perls, working with one person in the 'hot seat,' while other people paid

attention to their own reactions, and gave feedback about their experience afterwards. I think there are far more possibilities to Gestalt groupwork than this; yet it is important not to throw away this possibility. There are some situations where working with an individual group member is particularly useful for both the individual and the group. A group member might be isolating herself from other members, and may need the mediating function of the therapist to risk making contact with them; or might need the intensity of focus that the therapist might bring; or might be in a fragile state where only the therapist has the skills to provide appropriate contact; or might be setting up a situation where the group members will reject them. The individual might also be enacting a theme which has meaning for the whole group, which can be explored by the group through the work of the individual.

Example:

Jill: (Eyes defocused, silent)

Peter: What's happening for you, Jill?

Jill: (Still looking down) I'm scared. I think people will not want me in the group.

Peter: What is it about you in particular that we won't want you?

Jill: Other people are friends with each other. They talk to each other, but don't talk to me.

Peter: Can you think of any way in which you might contribute to that?

Jill: I don't know . . . I don't look at people much.

We can explore how Jill keeps others at a distance, all the while assuming they are distancing her. Later, Jill might get a sense of what she fears if she gets closer, and might risk some tentative contact. The group may also be confronted with its patterns of inclusion and exclusion.

3. *Exploring group process*

My colleague John Harris has pointed out (Philippson & Harris, 1992) that, by a strict observance of the 'Gestalt rule' that 'we' statements be turned into 'I' or 'you' statements, "The whole area of group process that focuses on the group as a whole is ignored or distorted." It becomes either a disguised 'I' statement — a projection — or a covert 'you' statement, avoiding naming someone.

The skillful question is how to hold to the importance of these 'I' and 'you' statements, and still acknowledge that the 'whole' of the group is more than the sum of its members. The group has rules, norms and culture, ways of responding to challenge, ways of dealing with difficulties and ways of celebrating. This is an important part of the field in which the individuals show themselves. By allowing an exploration of how the group operates, we can open the door to members acting to challenge this and take ownership of how they want the group to be.

INDIVIDUAL THERAPY AS GROUP THERAPY

The human organism/environment is, of course, not only physical but social. So in any humane study, such as human physiology, psychology, or psychotherapy, we must speak of a field in which at least social-cultural, animal, and physical factors interact. Our approach in this book is 'unitary' in the sense that we try in a detailed way to consider every problem as occurring in a social-animal-physical field. From this point of view, for instance, historical and cultural factors cannot be considered as complicating or modifying conditions of a simpler biophysical situation, but are intrinsic in the way any problem is presented to us. (PHG)

I would like to propose the concept that **all individual therapy is also group therapy.**

If I sit with an individual client, that client is not only presenting himself, but also the entire field of his interactions:
Family (parents, lover, children)
Community (neighborhood, work, friends)
Culture (family, neighborhood, national, world)

As the client progresses in therapy, so the client's interaction with his environment changes (in fact, in Gestalt terms the two statements are synonymous). Changes in the individual mirror and are mirrored in changes in the environment. A lasting change in the individual can only go hand-in-hand with changes in that individual's environment. These environmental changes happen in one of five different ways (I will give examples from the family environment, but this can also happen in the workplace or the community): 1. The environment rejects the individual and continues roughly as before. A family may switch roles around to replace the function of the individual as, for example, the "problem" or the "sick person" or the "person who looks after us." Sometimes, holding the "scapegoat" at a distance will be enough for the family to maintain business as usual. 2. By a mixture of compliments (on "how you used to be") and threats ("You'll be sorry"), the environment can reinduct the individual into previous ways of living. What the therapist sees in this situation is a client saying "All this therapy is fine in theory, but doesn't apply in the real world." 3. The individual client can leave a therapy session and dump his stored anger on others (e.g. parents, children, bosses) in the name of expressing feelings. This might lead to family rejection, or problems at work, or even abusive behavior towards children. If the client has the role of being the "problem person" in the family, this role would be strengthened by such a reaction. 4. The environment can also change to incorporate the change in the individual. This can happen very beautifully and spontaneously, as interpersonal problems seem to vanish where once they were overwhelming: Parents start showing their affection for their grown-up children; children stop "attention seeking" behaviors as they discover they are getting more attention anyway; work teams start functioning smoothly, and the previous splits no longer seem so important. 5. Sometimes the individual therapy client and her environment reach a compromise. For example, a 25 year old "child" leaves her parents' home to live independently. She maintains contact with her parents however, and chooses to accept some of the culture this involves (being seen as a child at times, accepting that her parents will put energy into their own conflicts rather than into their relationship with her). She has chosen out of a realistic assessment of what kind of relationship is available to her, preferring this to no relationship at all.

If individual therapy does not take into account the therapy of the whole environment, it is much more likely that the more destructive of these interactions will take place: i.e. the individual will be rejected by (or will reject) those who formerly were closest to him; or the individual will find himself slipping back into old patterns which fit more comfortably into others' expectations. Either way, the therapist's splitting of the individual/environment field will very likely be mirrored in the client's own process.

So, what are the ways of working with the whole field while doing individual therapy?

As I have discussed above, working with the individual inevitably *does* affect that individual's environment. Sometimes, shock waves go through the environment just from the individual's decision to go into therapy! People perceive themselves to be under scrutiny, and react with soul-searching, guilt, sometimes decisions to change stuck situations.

It is usually useful to "chart" the process of the environmental field around the client, to check out how others are reacting to the client's process, and how the client is responding to those reactions. This often becomes an important part of therapy, as the client risks relating differently with parents, partner, children, friends, people at work, authority figures — and they learn to act differently towards the client.

As well as discussing or role-playing these interactions, it is often interesting to "sculpt" families or situations. In a group, this can be done by psychodrama. In individual therapy, it can be done via a drawing, dialogues with cushions, or other kinds of sculpt. I use a pack of cards — the client chooses one card to represent each family member ("family" being interpreted loosely). The client then sculpts the family using the cards. One of the beauties of using cards is the many different ways of expressing similarity, difference, comparison and positioning. There are suit, color, card value, court cards, gender of Jack, Queen and King, positioning beside and positioning on top. For example, which family members are the same suit as the client? Often the family will fall into two suits, one mother's suit, one father's suit. Is somebody "between" the client and somebody else? Why is mother a King and father a Queen?

By one or a combination of these methods, the individual client is encouraged to see herself in terms of relationship to an environment.

I sometimes offer to run family or couple sessions (or sessions with ex-lovers) including individual clients.

I do not find difficulty in these circumstances with issues of "who has my first loyalty?." I come to the situation with the strong belief that loyalty to the individual client *is synonymous with* loyalty to the client's environment. This fits in well with the Gestalt focus: I am not trying to *fix* the client's situation (potentially at someone else's expense); I am working with *awareness*, which operates at the contact boundary between me and my client, between my client and her environment. I believe that this will allow for the best self-regulation for the client *and* the environment.

A potentially destructive aspect of working with different people in a couple or a family or a group of friends is if I get caught in a bind of confidentiality. I know that John is having an affair with Jenny while acting jealously towards his wife, Jan. Meanwhile Jan is having an affair with . . . This does not only happen in soap operas! My rule is that I am open to see husbands, wives, lovers, parents, children, either together with the client or (if agreed by both) separately — but I will not guarantee to keep confidentiality. Neither will I gossip about one to the other. Exploring issues around this rule is often enough in itself to unlock a situation clamped rigid by secrecy. I have never had a problem about this way of working since I stopped guaranteeing confidentiality — the problem once again becomes one for the client and his environment to resolve. And a surprising number of people do take up the option: Ex-lovers, parent and grown-up child, people in conflict.

We can bring other people into the therapy situation by empty cushions, with the client exploring different ways of relating to the other and her fantasies of their reactions (mixed with her own fears!). It is important to notice once again that I am not doing this as a behavioral tool to merely 'try something new out.'

While we are doing this, once again I am getting a sense not only of the individual and the person on the cushion, but the feel of the *kind of interactions* that take place within that family or whatever. Is there a lot of pleading, guilt-tripping, energy or lack of it, is it isolated from the community, are the expectations success or failure? This level is often at least as important as the individual level. The client is then exploring not only new ways of relating to the individual, but, *on behalf of the family*, exploring new ways of that family being in the world.

I want clients to clarify with whom they are angry, and what the unmet need or want now is. I make clear to the client that anger is a *contact* emotion, aiming towards improving contact. This is the dilemma for many children, when they express anger towards parents and, rather than ending in a more contactful relationship, their parents withdraw and denounce them as "bad." Later on, they want to sort out their relationship with Mum and Dad, and immediately feel overwhelmed with fear that anger will destroy that relationship. This may be partially true! Some parents will still not accept any expression of anger towards them, even more so thirty years' pent up rage.

I encourage clients to *negotiate* new relationships with those around them, especially parents, lovers and children. It may not be possible to achieve a relationship, and I see it as quite valid for clients to make compromises for the sake of a relationship that is important to them, *unless* that relationship requires that they give up a large proportion of their selfhood. They have the chance to show me their full feelings in therapy, and will often transferentially show whatever rage they experience towards me.

Gil Boyne, a hypnotherapist who also trained with Fritz Perls, links this with the 'Gestalt Prayer.' He emphasizes the line: "You are not in this world to live up to my expectations." This implies letting both yourself and your parents off the hook, rather than waiting for them to change before changing oneself. Boyne has also rewritten the last two lines of the 'Gestalt Prayer' very beautifully (Workshop Presentation, January 1989):

"If we meet as loving adults, that'll be wonderful;

If not, I'll accept that too, because that's the way it is."

I try and achieve a minimal distinction between therapy and the outside world. This is one of the reasons I prefer working with groups rather than working individually. However, even in individual therapy there are choices which can be made. I avoid great emphasis on confidentiality, safety and protection as "issues" in themselves. Rather, I want the client to be clear what his personal wants and needs are. What is the danger against which you need protection? What kind of protection can I provide? Who might it be important that you tell about yourself? Are you using issues of protection as an indirect way of getting me to confirm that you are helpless? I confront ways the client messes up the relationship with me and with others in a direct, caring, yet not overprotective manner. I want to communicate at the same time that he will not be destroyed by confrontation, and that I won't hurt him, not out of therapeutic choice but because why the hell should I? If I am gentle, it is because I get no pleasure out of hurting people, not because I have introjects of "protection."

HOW FAR CAN I TAKE THIS APPROACH?

The only real limit to this approach is: What connections are fully present here and now for me and my client? How far can I introduce questions about "What is my place in the nation, world, universe . . . ?" without sounding like a second-rate mystic? Whatever level we explore must connect with my client's (and my) own experience.

I shall give some examples:

1. *Martha* has been working on issues relating to abuse and neglect as a child. She has become aware of and expressed rage to her parents. Then:

Martha: They weren't all bad, you know.

Peter: Tell me about them.

Martha: Mother's parents were violent and distant. Her mother was always angry. My father's mother was very powerful, father didn't have anything to say for himself when she was about. It was just like he was with mother.

Peter: Abusive behavior often is handed down in this way. We're working to exorcize a demon, but not a demon called mum or dad. This demon is passed on generation to generation till someone says

"The buck stops here." Your anger is on behalf of all those who suffered from the demon.

Next session

Martha: I talked to my mum, said what we'd talked about, the demon and that, and she talked about her grandparents. We felt closer than we've been for years.

2. Jim has been working towards acknowledging his homosexuality.

Jim: But people won't accept me if I'm openly gay.

Peter: That'll sometimes be true.

We go on to discuss anti-gay prejudice, AIDS fears, how gay people can be accepted for themselves even if their sexuality is frowned on, gayness in other cultures: Ancient Greek, American Indian, and other positive gay images.

Peter: And you have choices. To be prepared to be openly gay doesn't mean you have to say it in the first sentence when you meet someone. You might want to, as a political statement, and it's a choice.

Jim: I guess I saw it as all or nothing. Come to think of it, I don't even know whether you're gay or straight.

Peter: I'll tell you if you want to know.

Jim: I realize it doesn't really matter to me.

3. *Karen* presents herself as depressed.

Karen: I feel very small and insignificant.

Peter: There's a big important universe out there, and then there's you.

Karen: Everything will go on just fine without me. I may as well not be here.

Peter: You're the left-over cog from when the universe was made.

Karen: Yes, like I was an "afterthought" in my family, 10 years younger than my brother. No-one really had time for me.

Peter: They didn't want you around. And neither did the rest of the universe?

Karen: No they didn't . . . Well, I suppose I didn't give them much chance.

Peter: So the cog says to the universe "Keep out"!

Karen: (Laughs) Something like that!

4. *Phil* is worried about his son *Mark*, 8 years old.

Phil: He says to me, "I hate you" and runs away. I don't know what I've done, I'm not violent or anything.

Peter: How do you feel when he says that?

Phil: Angry, sad.

Peter: What do you do or say to him?

Phil: Nothing. He wants to be on his own.

Peter: Be Mark.

Phil (M): I hate you dad. Go away.

Peter: How do you feel, Mark, when you say that?

Phil (M): Angry, sad, lonely.

Peter: What do you want from dad?

Phil (M): I don't know. I want him to leave me in peace.

Peter: And yet you're lonely. What would happen if he came closer instead?

Phil (M): I feel frightened. Maybe he'd hit me.

Peter: Is that what you want?

Phil (M): Well, maybe it's what I deserve.

Peter: For ... ?

Phil (M): For saying I hate him.

Peter: Anything else?

Phil (M): For pushing him away and making him angry.

Peter: So you push him away, otherwise he may hit you for pushing him away ... What if he hugged you instead?

Phil (M): I'd cry. I'd be cross with dad for making me cry.

Peter: So, Phil, what do you think?

Phil: I think I need to hug him.

Peter: He'll be frightened, angry and struggle.

Phil: Yes, well, we have to start somewhere!

Next session

Phil: The little tiger really fought me, but we ended up hugging, both of us in tears. Mother thought I was being cruel, but I kept on and Mark said "It's OK mum."

Peter: Mark got what he wanted and was scared to get . . . Now be mum!
(Now the locus of the conflict has shifted to the relationship between the parents. We need to work through all these shifts for therapy to be more than moving the conflict around. I may have sessions with the whole family, or may work with Phil and his wife, or just with Phil. Whichever way, I work with the whole family.)

Ethically, I am responsible not only for the therapy I do with the individual, but the therapy I do with the whole field. My goal is not to shift problems around, but to catalyze exploration and change in the environment at all levels towards greater contact and flexibility.

This may seem grandiose, and some parts of our environment are less open to change than others, but my experience is that change *does* happen in surprising places when this approach is taken.

It is also important ethically to differentiate what I have been saying from attempts to *manipulate* the environment. Therapy is a *contractual* undertaking. My client is my client. However, it is important to remember that the environment *is* affected, and that we cannot just disclaim response-ability for that (or its feedback effect on our client). Gestalt therapy fits this understanding well, with its emphasis on person-in-environment, and its avoidance of providing ready-made answers to the client. What we do is help the client — and through the client help his or her environment — to pose the questions that lead to fuller awareness of how they interact.

CONCLUSION

In looking at groups from a Gestalt field perspective, we can see them as rich arenas for both exploration and experimentation around the formation of self — both the self of the member individuals and the self of the group. We have seen that, as the individual is inseparable from her environmental field, all individual therapy can be looked at from the perspective of group therapy.

In the next chapter, I shall apply this approach to particular kinds of groups: couples and families.

Chapter 11

WORKING WITH COUPLES
AND FAMILIES

A very particular kind of group which therapists often work with is the family grouping, which could range from a couple in a committed relationship (whether or not married or cohabiting) to an extended family with children and grandparents. The most common approach to this kind of work is to discover and alter the *systemic* interactions between members of the family or couple. These approaches have been imported and assimilated by various Gestaltists: See, for example, Zinker (1994); or Hunter Beaumont's assimilation of Hellinger's 'Order of Love' approach.

My aim here is to talk about my experience in working with couples and families using the Gestalt *field* approach I have been developing in this book. Of course, some assumptions are common to both systems and field approaches. My assumptions within this approach are:

1. That it is not possible to understand adequately any individual (including the therapist) except in relation to that person's presently important environment (which will include the individual's significant relationships).

2. The paradoxical theory of change: It is not my aim to change the couple's or family's behavior. By doing so, I would be buying into their sense of their behavior being out of their control and needing some outsider to alter it for them. I would aim rather to explore what is, and what processes support the observable behavior of the couple or family, who can then take ownership of their behavior and change it if they so wish.

3. In the therapeutic situation, the therapist is also a significant part of the family's environment. The therapist is therefore not merely an external consultant to the family, as Zinker also believes, but an integral part of all the interactions taking place within the therapy room. Furthermore, what the therapist sees is not 'the family,' but how the family shows itself in the presence of the therapist.

4. My function is not to achieve any particular result, but to join the couple or family in their exploration of their relationships. My approach is phenomenological, staying as much as possible with the obvious rather than interpretations. I need to be particularly aware with couples and families that any interpretations I make may be wrong, since these develop their own way of communicating which often does not have the usual meaning. Also, following what I said in 3. above, my interpretation will be based on how the family shows itself to me, not necessarily how the family is elsewhere.

5. While I do not hold a brief to keep a family or couple together or push them apart, I give a value to *commitment*. Not breaking up a relationship at the first signs of difficulty.

I shall say more about each of these. I use the general term 'family' to cover couple relationships also, unless otherwise stated.

SELF-ACTUALIZATION IN THE FAMILY

The basic Gestalt field orientation is that selfhood is maintained by the ego functions of identification and alienation. I am configuring myself in relation to what is other. Family relationships (whether it be family of origin or families formed in adulthood) can thus be characterized by the operation of these functions. In what ways do I configure myself by my identification with my family: Values, commitments, ways of doing things, attitudes? In what ways do I configure myself by alienation from other family members: Areas of disagreement, separation, conflict? These identifications and alienations will also be integrated into my personality function, or self-concept.

It is important to understand that families are a vital source of self-orientation by means of both these functions. Furthermore, this process is a mutual one, because other family members will also be self-orienting in relation to me. In our mutual self- and other-configuration, what we could call the 'family-self' is formed, and achieves its own ways of stabilizing itself, or homoeostasis.

A GESTALT VIEW OF FAMILY HOMOEOSTASIS

I have spoken before about homoeostasis, and the distinctive Gestalt way of understanding this. In systemic family therapy in particular, homoeostasis is seen as how the family stays the same, how it stays disordered. To quote Palazzoli et al (1978), for example: "The schizophrenic game and homoeostasis are, in fact, synonymous . . . ." In Gestalt therapy, homoeostasis is understood as a companion pole to creativity, acting in partnership to accommodate to a changing organism/environment field. The homoeostasis we look at is not merely the homoeostasis within the family, but within the whole field.

Thus, rather than talking about fixed people acting in a fixed way, we are looking at a fluid, changing field, out of which individual and family selves emerge and stabilize themselves in the changing field. Yet people and families can feel overwhelmed by the very fluidity of this process, especially if they have had painful experiences of the wider field (or the family story is of the dangers outside the family), and act to maintain a predictable and surviv-able structure under all circumstances. This now looks more like the systemic view of homoeostasis. What Gestalt adds, as it does to the view of individual neurotic behavior, is an understanding of the fragility of this predictability, and the hard work the family must put in at all times to maintain it.

The basis of the fragility of the neurotic homoeostasis is the changeability of the field in which the family exists and makes its relationships. In fact, with the presence of the therapist in the family, the field has already changed. The only ways in which the family can keep their patterns afloat are by inducting the therapist into the family pattern or leaving therapy. I can thus ask all the questions I ask of the client and myself at the beginning of individual therapy: What are their expectations of me, how do they want me to see and respond to them, how do I feel in their presence, etc. I make sure that I do not become confluent with their pattern, but keep my separateness and choicefulness. At the same time, I need to show my commitment to and acceptance of the family, or they will just leave.

If I can be an other that is not confluent with the family pattern, yet values them and shows interest in their process, and their anxieties and expectations which support the process, then the creative aspect of homoeostasis can find a new balance, and thus a new self-actualization of the family. This is the 'paradoxical theory of change' as it applies to families.

It is important to note that this is not the paradox of the systemic therapists such as Haley (1971) or Palazzoli et al (1978) (the 'Milan School'). Their use of paradox is a strategy, otherwise called "prescribing the symptom," whereby the therapist takes on the role of supporting the behavior, and even of exaggerating it, to allow the family to move into the counter-role of developing new possibilities. The Gestalt paradox is not about manipulation, but about starting where the client (individual, couple, family, group) is, and thus bringing ownership and choice back to their function-ing.

Example

I am working with a couple, Dora and Jim.

J: (To Dora) When I come home from work, you never stop what you're doing to say hello. I feel unwelcome, a nuisance.

D: You expect me to stop what I'm doing instantly. When I don't, you go to the living room in a huff and don't talk to me.

P: What do you do then, Dora?

D: I just say "Sod him," and go back to what I was doing.

P: What interests me most is that you both seem to react quickly to the other one's unavailability. How you react is to withdraw angrily. I guess it would make it difficult for you to relate together unless you both want the same thing at the same time.

J: Well, I just think that a simple welcome never hurt anyone.

P: I'm wondering whether you are feeling annoyed with me.

J: Well yes, to be honest. This is such a simple courtesy, yet you make it more complicated.

P: What I want to hold onto is that this all seems much more significant to you both than a simple matter of courtesy. Somehow, it sounds as if there is something important enough that you between you make Jim's homecoming a source of discomfort. I am also aware that you both state the matter in ways which make it difficult to discuss or compromise.

D: Well, Jim wants it his own way, and that's that.

P: And the other side is that you are damned if you will give him his own way!

What I am doing here is staying with the theme that the couple brings, without trying to resolve it. In individual therapy with either Doris or Jim, I might explore how the client and I first come together at the start of a session, or what a lack of welcome means to the client. In couples therapy, I avoid looking too much at individual processes, and prefer to stay with the interactions. Unlike other groups I work with therapeutically, I do not have an individual therapy contract with people in couples and families. I do not want to buy into "We'll be OK if you are different." The point is rather to find a way of these people communicating with the others *as they are*.

Here there seems to be a fight between Jim and Doris over how to define this situation. They are trying to draw me in to support one side or another, which I will not do. Rather, I let the theme develop. Of course, there might be something analogous that occurs when a therapy session with me begins. Do they leave me space to enter with my own interests or wishes, or continue what they are doing?

THE THERAPIST IS PART OF THE PROCESS

Looking back at the dialogue between Doris and Jim above, we can see how the context of couple with therapist sets the scene for what occurs. They want me as therapist to support their perspective, so they complain about each other. If I do support one side or another, or by my interventions with either make it look as if I see something uniquely 'wrong' with one partner, then their stuck way of dealing with the situation is untouched, and the therapy is neutralized. As I stay out of this confluence, and proclaim my interest in what they are doing together, the fact of my presence and my interest creates a new situation for the couple to deal with.

I also need to remember that what is said is not necessarily 'true.' Often the complaints made by one person about another are wild generalizations, or interpretations of what the other person is doing which bear little resemblance to how the other person would describe her actions. They will be seeing me as someone to tell their troubles to, and thus will be configuring their interactions as troublesome.

However, my starting point is that, whatever motivates each individual, if the family's actions lead again and again to a result which they do not like, something interesting is happening if they continue with the actions rather than find some new way of relating. If Jim is motivated to want an immediate welcome home by his assumptions of how wives are with husbands from his family of origin, he is still making the choice not to discuss this amicably with Doris in order to avoid the unpleasantness of his return home.

THE IMPORTANCE OF PHENOMENOLOGY

More than in any other kind of therapy, the meanings I assign to a family's actions and presentation are likely to be inaccurate. Each family can be seen as a cultural entity in its own right, with its own customs, and even its own language. As much as possible, I must stay with what I observe, rather than the significance I put on that observation. The systemic therapists put this very well (sometimes better than their Gestalt imitators):

> We had also been conditioned by the linguistic model, according to which the predicate we link to the subject becomes an inherent quality of that subject while, in effect, it is no more than a function of the relationship. For example, if a patient

appeared to be sad, we concluded he was sad, and we went to far as to try and understand why he was sad, inviting and encouraging him to speak to us about his sadness . . .

For example, if, during a heated argument between her husband and son, Mrs. Rossi seemed bored and faraway, it was a mistake to conclude that she really was bored, and to discuss and try to discover the reason for that boredom. Instead, we found it more productive to silently observe the effects of her behavior on the others in the group, ourselves included. (Palazzoli et al, 1978, italics in original)

This is a very important consideration in family work (and often in individual therapy as well). I also want to point out the vital addition "ourselves included." If I can keep my own grounding and my phenomenological bracketing, there is a possibility of much useful therapy.

Example

John and Karen, and their 6-year-old son Bruce, have come to therapy primarily because of the "behavior problems" of their son. In the session, Bruce looks angry, makes faces at people and 'blows raspberries.'

K: You see what we have to put up with! He's a little horror. We've tried everything, and he won't stop.

J: He deserves a bloody good hiding. You wait till I get you home.

I am noticing that all the relating is via Bruce, who is grinning. This may have more to do with the way his parents react to his expression than with his joy.

P: OK Bruce, you've got my attention — now what?

Bruce looks uncertain. John and Karen look shocked. I look at Bruce in silence, he looks at me.

K: Come on Bruce, tell the man why you're being such a nuisance.

J: What's the use, he's just a little terror.

P: What I'm noticing is that none of you seem to get a clear run at saying what you want to say without interruption. Bruce interrupts parents, parents interrupt Bruce. I wonder if any of you would want a go at just saying how things are for you while others listen? Nobody needs to interrupt: you can have time yourself afterwards.

Long silence!

In this extract, I am not working from a reductionist premise (they are doing this just in order to interrupt), but with the orientation that my focus is on the activity of the family group as a whole rather than an individual. I suggest an experiment, which will be a valid experiment whether or not they "do it." The silence in itself is a new response to a new opportunity.

DO I ENCOURAGE THE FAMILY/COUPLE TO STAY TOGETHER?

Different couples and family therapists bring different perspectives to this question. Some bring the value that children need both parents, and they suffer more if parents separate than from almost any conflict involved in them staying together. Some bring the value: "If you are not happy, then change partners." I would like to come at the question obliquely, via my understanding of groups.

Recall that the way I have defined groups does not require people to meet. Also, recall that I wrote that "groups in a sense never end, and in another sense are always ending." From this perspective, the couple or family are working towards an ending of their present groupness; and, even if they separate, they are still a family grouping. Actually, separated families well illustrate this way of understanding groups. Often the group processes in such a family are well worth exploring! I have worked with separated couples in the past, and found this work useful.

Furthermore, if the aim of the work is to increase choicefulness (restoration of ego functions), it is usually obvious to the family that some kind of separation is one of the possible choices. If I discourage exploration of this choice, it might contribute to a sense of trappedness in the relationship, which itself might contribute to a walkout by a family member. Conversely, a focus on the end of what was in the past can be precisely what is needed to allow the formation of a new groupness which allows the couple or family to stay together.

Two illustrations come to me here: A client in a therapy group who announced that she was leaving. I acknowledged that she was free to leave, and my good wishes would go with her. She then said "In that case I don't have to leave." The other illustration is from a couple who had separated some time before, and were coming to see me together to explore where they were now. In the course of the work, they restarted their sexual relationship, then separated consensually and choicefully, knowing that this wasn't where they were now.

COMMITMENT

For the reasons I have just put, I do not take the stance of either the desirability of staying together or of separation (and from another perspective see the inevitability of both). However, nor do I encourage an easy ending of couple and family relationships. You could say that the stance I take is one I call 'not-quite-neutrality.' On the one hand, I am not putting myself forward as the authority figure who will decide what will happen with this couple. On the other hand, I am aware of a silent, but important, third partner in the relationship: The partners' commitment to the relationship.

Culturally, we are in a time when commitment is not a valued concept. Fritz Perls talked (Perls, 1969) about the "instant turner-onners." Looking around me, the emphasis everywhere seems to be on quick answers, lack of commitment to any structure, and an expectation that people will be willing to move at short notice to wherever the next bright idea wants them to be. New structural initiatives on the health service, education, transport, industry and economics are constantly being brought out. Each time this happens, a whole group of workers is redeployed or deprived of employment, or told to move to a new location. No sooner are people beginning to sort out the difficulties of one new structure than it is replaced again. Workers face the insecurity of knowing that there is a strong probability that their jobs will disappear at some random time. Similar jobs might even reappear with the next turn of the wheel, but not for them.

If commitment is not present in a relationship or an undertaking, then there is usually a great sense of insecurity, as any problem, discomfort, or disagreement immediately leads to the question "Is this the end?." The effort involved in working through these can be avoided by giving up, or giving in. In the latter case, I can go for a superficial agreement, and, while still seeming to be in the relationship, it is no longer the one that fulfills what I wanted from it.

When I work with couples like this, I suggest that they make an absolute commitment to staying together for, say, six months. In doing this, they often find that their relationship changes so that problems are more easily sorted out, and both people's needs are met. This does not mean that they necessarily stay together at the end of the six months: Some do, some do not. However, even if they decide to separate, they will be able to do so with a sense that they have first of all really worked to meet each other. A prerequisite for saying a proper goodbye is having said a proper hello first!

CONCLUSION

This chapter cannot be a full description of my approach to couples and family therapy. My hope is more to show that Gestalt field theory can be usefully applied in this arena. In this model, the way I work with couples and families is not essentially different from my work with individuals and groups, if I bear in mind that my 'client' is the relationship rather than the individuals, and the extra importance of a phenomenological approach rather than assuming I understand the meaning of what the family shows me.

Chapter 12

A GESTALT APPROACH
TO VALUES AND ETHICS

Gestalt therapy developed (in its Californian days in the late 1960s and early 1970s) in a cultural context where rules and moralities were being questioned and thrown away, where freedom was valued over law. Fritz Perls, and many who followed him, allowed themselves many freedoms which would usually be frowned on in psychiatry and psychotherapy. In particular, these Gestaltists went from their emphasis on the real relationship with the therapist, and consequent de-emphasis on transference, to a willingness to develop a therapeutic relationship into something else: A friendship, even a sexual relationship. Spontaneity was valued most highly in relating.

More recently, many Gestalt therapists have wanted more acceptance in the professional world, and this has often meant a wholesale acceptance of codes of ethics and ways of acting without taking personal ownership of the values adhered to. The codes have become for many a kind of introject, which have more to do with appearing professional than with assimilation. For Perls, this would have been truly unethical!

INTROJECTION AND ASSIMILATION: RULES AND VALUES

Gestalt therapy does in fact provide a useful basis for looking at personal and professional ethics. Recall the distinction made between an introject, an undigested lump of ways of functioning, and an assimilated way of being. In the latter, I will have 'chewed' the behavior, and made mine what is nourishing, while discarding that which is not nourishing. We can look at the same distinction in contrasting a personality function which is rigid and based on other people's rules; and a personality function of which I take ownership, and whose rules are open to me to update if I wish.

Gestalt therapy has something further to add. In a philosophy which understands 'self' as an internal process, there would be the immediate objection that such a self-chosen value system would be 'selfish.' I would be choosing what is nourishing for me and disregarding the needs of my fellows, or my environment. However, the emphasis in Gestalt therapy is on self as a relational process, arising at the contact boundary between me-organism and my environment, and sustained by both. Thus care of my environment is an unavoidable part of self-care.

Now I could get to another pole, of limiting my possibilities by an exaggerated concern for the environment. So it is important to say that I do not believe Gestalt therapy supports this either. The Gestalt view of homoeostasis emphasizes the importance of linking the concept with creativity and the willingness to risk one's self contactfully. The attempt to rigidly sustain any balance is in itself destructive of balance. In risking myself, on this Gestalt view, I must also be willing to risk the environment, but again contactfully.

A Gestalt Approach to Values and Ethics

A Gestalt Theory of Values

I believe that what I have sketched above is the basis for a subtle and balanced system of values and personal ethics. This system has its own 'commandments,' and I shall now suggest what these are:

1. *Take responsibility for being yourself*

Own your actions, your responses, your choices, your place in the world. Do not act as if you are merely the victim of other people, your past, your genes, the political system. If you give in to *force majeur*, be aware that it is your choice. Be aware: Awareness is my ownership of my choosing.

2. *Know that self grows from contact*

You cannot be yourself while enclosed in a fantasy world. Self means nothing without other. Without concern for the other, you cannot properly care for yourself.

3. *Risk yourself in creative encounter with the world*

Any attempt to control yourself or your environment down a well-trodden path is likely to lead to a destruction worse than the one you are trying to avoid. Accept anxiety: The alternative is worse!

4. *Be honest*

Do not create an image of yourself other than how you are. If you do, the environment will nourish your image rather than you. If you lie, lie with awareness and integrity, rather than with self-deception and cynicism.

5. *Accept that things go wrong*

Don't be over-careful: It won't stop things going wrong sometimes. All you will do is progressively limit your choices, so that, when things do go wrong, you will find it difficult to ride out the troubles.

GESTALT PROFESSIONAL ETHICS

Let us try and relate these commandments to professional ethics. I would like to bite the bullet, and illustrate this with the ethical stance of our founder, Fritz Perls. I believe that he exemplified many of these values. He risked himself in his contact with others, accepting people's love and rejection, tenderness and (sometimes even murderous) rage. He was honest: It is important to realize that what distinguished Perls in his sexual relating with clients from many in other therapeutic systems was not so much that he engaged in such relationships — so did, for example, Jung and Reich and many others in the psychotherapy world — but that he was open about it. I do not want to get too caught up here in the area of sexual ethics, but it has been a source of controversy about Gestalt therapy, and needs to be addressed.

Where I believe that Perls may have lost sight of the ethics implicit in his creation was that he became confluent with 'Fritz Perls the Gestalt therapist.' In other words, he fell into the trap of many therapeutic and spiritual teachers, that he stopped allowing himself to deal with the world in any other way. The people he met were eventually all clients, trainees, disciples, or hangers-on. He had to be either celibate or have sex with them. He seems to me to have had no other interests (whether ballroom dancing or chess or sitting in the local bar as one of the regulars with people who didn't know that he was 'the Fritz Perls') through which he met people on an equal level.

The major reason I would not get involved in a sexual relationship with a client or a trainee is that clients and trainees only know me in a specific context, which I would not want to live up to. By this latter, I do not just mean that the client transfers onto me projections of parental and other important figures (although this is true, as is the fact that erotic feelings about clients can have a wider significance than the obvious). I also mean that when I am with the client, I am there in support of their needs, not to get my own needs met. In my personal relationships, I want to be able to meet needs both ways, to be uninterested in the other person at times, to be able, as a last resort, to end a relationship which I do not find nourishing for me. Furthermore, the client would not be showing me many aspects of his behavior: I rarely know what music, food, or films clients like, and only have a general sense of how they like to enjoy themselves.

I think that there would be very little connection between a good therapeutic or training relationship and this kind of relationship, and the need for unlearning both ways would make the previous relationship a disadvantage rather than an advantage. By choice, I have close and important relationships outside the psychotherapy world, and this is the appropriate place for getting my own needs met.

So, my adaptation of the general ethical principles to professional ethics is:

1. *Responsibility*

I must own my responsibility for what happens in the therapy room. I am a responsible partner in all that occurs, including how the client is. This means that I do not merely turn everything that happens back to the client, but acknowledge to myself, and where appropriate to the client, my part in events. I must be willing to apologize for my part in mismeetings.

The other side of this is that I do not give up my power in the therapy situation. If I do this out of a wish to protect the client, I also make it impossible for the client to fully express her own responsibility. Nor do I force my power on the client, nor move away when the encounter becomes uncomfortable for me.

I must also leave the responsibility for the client's life essentially with the client. I must not require the client to give me authority over her life or relationships (except sometimes very temporarily to prevent serious harm). I must not require the client to see me as a parental figure or herself as a child in relation to me. I have responsibility for the damaging mistakes I have made in my own life, and the client must have similar responsibility, unless she is demonstrably so out of contact that she cannot take that responsibility, which is very rare.

2. *Be available for contact*

I must not hide my presence behind my expertise or techniques such as experiments. To the extent that either of these help someone to move to a new edge, he must find me there at the edge in order to support the novelty.

3. *Be willing to risk yourself*

It can be very easy for a therapist to stay with a client in the safe area where both are relatively comfortable and unchallenged. At worst, the therapy stagnates. At best, the client gets affirmation, which can be very easily undone by the weight the client can give to the next critical remark that someone makes. I need rather to be willing at any moment to risk moving off confluent tramlines onto a track that more fully expresses our interaction as autonomous human beings.

4. *Be honest*

I must not deceive myself for my own comfort, nor for my clients 'for their own good.' If I am stuck with a client, or feel awkward about some aspect of our relating, I must find an appropriate way to face this, usually with the client, sometimes with myself. I particularly need to be emotionally honest, not surrounding myself with a blanket aura of 'warmth' or affection, but open to what the actuality of my feelings (or lack of feelings) are with this particular client at this particular time.

I must also not make a rule or a technique of honesty, saying everything that I feel the moment I feel it. I must stay as

212

much as possible honestly aware of what I feel, and share what furthers the therapy, i.e. what the client can chew on and assimilate.

5. *Accept that things go wrong*

I must be forgiving of myself, while at the same time willing to question myself and expand my abilities. I must avoid being the 'perfect therapist,' nor idealize others as perfect therapists or trainers. Thus I know that I will at times fall short in all the 'musts,' including this one. I need to notice the areas where I fall short, and have enough excitement in my work to wish to improve in these areas. I cannot be an effective Gestalt therapist without this excitement running like a thread through my work, though, of course, not feeling it all the time.

I believe that these ethical principles are both necessary and sufficient for a Gestalt psychotherapist. They can be expanded into more formal language, but any extension can be a detraction from the existential core of Gestalt therapy.

Chapter 13

ENDING

Now that we are open and vulnerable together, we can end. Old questions arise anew. Can I get along without you? Will it hurt? Have I been exploited? I am free, but can I stand it alone? Each of us experiences a recapitulation of the fears and hopes we had in the beginning. I want to end in accordance with my needs and my boundaries, and want you to do the same. This will be a new kind of ending, one that is finished, at least for now. So let us express our doubts, fears, and gratitudes — whatever is necessary to make a complete experience this time. (Arnold Beisser in "Gestalt Evaluation: Individual Case Study" [unpublished]).

BASIC ASSUMPTIONS

In psychotherapies based on symptom-removal, the criteria for ending therapy are fairly straightforward: Either the symptom goes, or therapist, client, or both decide that the therapy will not remove the symptom. In Gestalt therapy, based on exploration of the client's self-process, we must go beyond these simpler notions.

We need to go back to basic assumptions. For, while we are not out to 'fix' the client, we have a theoretical assumption that what we do will be helpful to the client. We know that most clients do wish that their lives will be enriched by the time, commitment and money they spend in therapy, so we would not be doing Gestalt therapy in good faith if we do not believe — and check out — that what we do is theoretically and practically capable of delivering this. I will go through some basic assumptions of Gestalt therapy as I see them, as an introduction to the ending process.

It is fitting that we go back to the beginning, to our first principles, as part of exploring endings. Questions for endings must include "What have we done?," "Have I got what I wanted?," "What have we not done?": Questions which must include an overview of what it was we set out to do in the first place, as a context for what we have actually done.

1. *Everybody hurts sometimes* (REM song)

As an existential therapy, Gestalt does not hold out the hope that we will be happy all the time, or that things will not go wrong again, or that bad things will not happen to us. We can in fact guarantee that the rough and the smooth will continue to co-exist. In fact, we could usually assume that if someone's life was permanently smooth, it would be by insulating themselves from the fullness of contact with the world, avoiding the difficulties and commitments inherent in real relating, and, often, exporting the difficulties to those with whom they come into contact.

Thus termination (and beginning) of Gestalt therapy is not necessarily linked to how difficult the client's life is. People's lives do not need to be falling apart to come into therapy, nor problem-free for them to leave.

2. *Moving from manipulating the environment for support to self-support*

I have written earlier about this original statement by Perls of the aim of Gestalt therapy. This is speaking about two different 'knacks' for dealing with the ups and downs of life. The knack learned in a hostile environment, particularly in childhood, is to act in such a way as to avoid unwelcome attention, show yourself in such a way that people look after you, or avoid you, or at least do not hurt you too often. It would not be part of that knack to go directly for what you want or need, or respond directly to other people's ants or needs.

Contact is replaced by mutual manipulation.
 The knack regarded by Gestalt therapy as a human being's natural state is to start by contacting the environment, then aggress on that environment and let it aggress on you. Thus in a hostile environment I would either find part of the environment that is not hostile to me (move away), or act to make it less hostile (call the police, fight), or accept the hostility in support of a higher-priority need or commitment (feeding my family, learning something I value). I would be asserting my humanity by making choices moment by moment. I am orienting myself so that the environment can support me in these choices. This is 'self-support.' It is important to notice once again that this is not about doing it all for oneself. In fact, it is in this contactful and choiceful orientation in the organism/environment field that the flexible self of Gestalt therapy emerges.

3. *Moving from a chronic low-grade emergency to a high-grade but safe emergency*
 The image here (for which I thank Petruska Clarkson) is of coming to live with a stone in my shoe. I would develop hard skin to protect me to some extent from the stone and I would learn to walk so as to minimize the discomfort. However, in accepting the discomfort as an inseparable part of living, I would be accepting also reduced sensitivity in and awareness of my foot, and posture difficulties arising from an unbalanced way of walking.

The therapy would be to focus directly on the center of the discomfort, acknowledging that this actually hurts, and maybe choosing to stop, take off my shoe and remove the stone. On the level of self, I would stop identifying with the stone in my shoe, rather alienating it as not-me, and thus something I can reorientate myself in relation to.

Moving away from the illustration, what this amounts to is that the therapist supports and challenges the client to face the world with a higher level of courage and response-ability, and asserting her choicefulness in the face of difficulty.

HOW THERAPY ENDS

We are now ready to look at what this means for the termination of Gestalt therapy.

First of all, we need to acknowledge that not everyone wants what we are offering. Some want to be manipulated into specific behavior changes, such as to stop smoking, without facing any of these questions. It is important to be willing to be clear about what we are, and are not, offering. As the late Isadore From said, "You are not a department store, you are a boutique." If someone wants a type of therapy different from what I offer, I refer on. The point I am making here is that it is difficult to end a therapy well if we have not started well. We need to have a sense of completion of an enterprise in which we are both partners.

Once we have mutually agreed our way of working together, I will be monitoring with the client the development of self-support and the movement from chronic low-grade emergency to high-grade emergency in relation to which the client can act choicefully. Experientially, I will be meeting the client at a mutual energy level sufficient to support the work the client wishes to do. If I do not experience this over a period of time, I will raise with the client what is happening in our relationship.

At some stage, the answer to this will be that the client has relearned the knack of self-support sufficiently to stay choiceful and contactful in whatever difficulties he is currently experiencing, both in daily life and in relation to me. This is then the time to move towards an ending. Usually this is an agreed step between us. Sometimes a client will make an abrupt ending to avoid going further with something painful, or as a habitual way of avoiding endings. I would discourage this, as it does not seem helpful to end up with the therapy itself as a piece of 'unfinished business.' Of course, the final decision will be with the client.

Occasionally, the client will verbally wish to continue, while not acting in accordance with our contract. This might involve breaking our contractual agreements on violence or payment, or refusal to take responsibility for their own process and relying on me to 'fix' them. They may also merely be attending as a requirement of a course they are on, such as counseling or psychotherapy. In those circumstances, I would consider terminating the therapy unilaterally, allowing sufficient time for the client to make what ending she can with me, including expressing whatever anger she may feel about my termination of the therapy. I do not like doing this, but I would not be able to continue working in good faith with someone with whom I do not have a contractual understanding.

THE TASKS OF ENDING THERAPY

Even when therapist and client have acknowledged that their work together is ending, there are aspects of the ending process that need to be attended to before we stop. One of the paradoxes of therapy is that a deep and important relationship comes to an end precisely when it reaches its fullest contact. It is almost as if I am saying to the client, "I will only be in relation to you if you are in difficulty." Meanwhile the client is likely to have his own difficulties with saying a final goodbye. Questions that are often present for the client are: "Can I tolerate the pain of separation?," "Can I make it on my own?," "Can I come back if things go wrong?," "If not, does she care about me?" A question for both therapist and client is "Am I hanging onto the relationship because I don't want to lose the other (whether from emotional or commercial considerations). Just as at the beginning of therapy, the therapist's boundaries will be tested here, and the therapist will need to be very clear.

For me the tasks of ending are:

1. *Moving away from the therapy relationship*

Part of this will be to pull back somewhat from the relationship, and get an overall sense of what we have done together. What has changed or been addressed, what has stayed un-addressed? Are there any particular themes that have characterized the therapy, and what is the present state of play with these themes? What potentials for exploration between us are we agreeing not to open up?

We also need to be clear that the relationship is really ending. However much I as a therapist work to preserve the autonomy of the client, I will be a person to turn to, someone to listen, someone important in the client's life. The client is preparing for a life without me doing these things. For some clients, well connected in their own environment, this will be easy; for others, it will be difficult, and our ending will leave a hole which they will need to fill in some way. I will say more about this later.

One way of not having an ending is to make it an *au revoir*, till we meet again, or till I need you again. I do not accept such an ending. I tell clients that we may or may not meet again, we may or may not even work together again, but that we are not ending on that basis. The relationship really is ending, without any expectations that it will restart. If a client is not willing to take on that understanding of our ending for herself, I will unilaterally say that I will not under any circumstances work with her again. We could then work through the client's response to this, while I clarify that for me this is not a rejection but a holding of a clear boundary on which the tasks of ending can take place.

I relate similarly to letters after our ending. I will read letters from ex-clients where I do not get the sense that they are trying to restart the relationship. If I do get that sense, I will ask them not to write again.

2. Moving away from the personal relationship

We also need to acknowledge and give time for the feelings involved in the dying of our personal relationship. These feelings could be of sadness, of joy, of fear, and/or of anger, depending on the situation, and the way the client configures the ending. The client will also want to know what the therapist is feeling, how the ending impacts the therapist.

I want to be able to end with all that is personal between us acknowledged, including regrets and frustrations.

3. Reorienting to facing the world without therapeutic support

A therapist is in some ways an easy person to be supported by. I will be reliable, not have too much of my own agenda, clear in my boundaries. To be willing to risk support elsewhere can be more difficult. Maybe the other person will be too busy, or want to talk about their own problems, or just give advice. And yet that is the stuff of everyday relationships, which can be avoided precisely by being in therapy. It is in this sense, of leaving a person who is contractually committed to the client's growth, that he is 'leaving home,' and facing the fear of that aloneness.

For some clients ('borderline'), therapy often finishes after they stop seeing me. Their experience (starting in infancy with their parents) is that attempts to achieve some independence are met with rejection. They thus either cling close (everything is good but suffocating) or run away (all is bad). My experience is that they often leave messily, either over-quickly, avoiding facing our ending together, or angrily, rejecting what we have achieved together. Often the ex-client then comes back, or writes or phones to leave more fully some time later.

In keeping with my approach throughout this book, I want to avoid describing a 'normal' or 'abnormal' ending process. We have an 'autonomous criterion': Is our final movement away from each other unified, lively, graceful, energetic, releasing? If not, there is something in the field of our contact which still needs to be attended to, if possible, before we part.

Gestalt theory identifies confluence as the most likely way of interrupting the ending of a contact (the post-contact phase). It is worthwhile looking out for attempts (by either client or therapist) to cling to the relationship.

So, in nearing the end this book, I am aware there are a number of tasks I need to complete before finishing: Editing, references, etc. Behind that, there are my fears about finishing: Will it be acceptable to a publisher; will people buy it; will they like it? There will also be the hole in my life where the book has been for several years. The ideas in the book have organized my thinking, teaching and conference presenting. So now what?!

In fact, I have become aware of new possibilities. I have offered a workshop on an entirely different subject for a conference, written a paper for a journal, arranged for supervision in America. I am ready to risk finishing the book.

And what about Jan, our fictitious/composite client?

J: I've been in my new relationship now for six months, and it's wonderful. I have friends, interests, many of the things I thought I'd never have. I feel very different.

P: You sound as if you are summing up the period of our therapy together. Is there something about us finishing in what you are saying?

J: I've actually thought about that. I guess the answer is yes, but every time I think about it I feel frightened. You feel very much a part of these changes: can I keep them up without you?

P: I hear echoes of what you said when you first came. Is this you acting in a different way, or following the lead of a different man: me? For me, I'd say it's you. You certainly haven't just done what I've told you to . But you will have to answer that question for yourself. It's not a question I can help you with, because of the nature of the question.

J: I see what you mean. Yes, I think I am ready to end . . . and I feel frightened again . . . and sad.

And so we go into our ending. I feel sad writing about this, remembering endings with clients, and thinking about endings to come.

In keeping with what I have said about the process of ending, I will sum up with a chapter giving an overview of Gestalt therapy as I have conceptualized it in this book.

Chapter 14

A MAP OF GESTALT THERAPY

Reading the literature, one of the major problems I find is that different writers use quite different words to describe Gestalt therapy (and sometimes use the same words to describe different things). There are all these words: field theory, existentialism, phenomenology, contact, awareness, self, ego, id, personality, dialogue, experiment, interruptions to contact, layers of neurosis . . . How do they fit together? Are they to be bolted onto each other, or do they stem from a more basic philosophical perspective?

I want to finish this book by presenting here my own map of Gestalt therapy, from its first principles in philosophy to its expression in specific methods of psychotherapy. This chapter is particularly geared to the Gestalt therapist, who wishes to get a sense of where I stand on various aspects of Gestalt theory. I am also keen to encourage others to make their own 'maps,' and show how the theory hangs together for them.

GROUND LEVEL: THE FIELD

Gestalt field theory begins with the whole. It is not that there are 'things' which contact other 'things,' but that "It is the contact that is the simplest and first reality." (PHG). This is stressed over and over again by PHG:

> ... it is always to such an interacting field that we are referring, and not to an isolated animal. Where the organism is mobile in a great field and has a complicated internal structure, like an animal, it seems plausible to speak of it by itself ... but this is simply an illusion ... "

Thus the definition of a human being is the definition of the person/environment field, and the creative adjustments that the person is making in the field. The process of adjustment in the field creates/defines the person as much as, or more than, the person defines the creative adjustment.

See chapter 2 for a more detailed exploration of Gestalt field theory.

EXISTENTIALISM AND PHENOMENOLOGY

Existentialism was a philosophical reversal of the dualism inherent in Platonic and Cartesian thought: Essence and matter, body and soul. Existentialism makes primary the 'is-ness' of existence, rather than any attributes. There is great emphasis on the choices which people make, and people's relationship with the givens of the world, for example with death. And this is precisely what Gestalt field theory offers. The field is primary, experience arises from the field, 'self ' and 'other' are processes in the field, our choices configure the field, meaning arises from field interactions rather than from some pre-existing 'essences.' Instead of Aristotle's "The unexamined life is not worth living," we have rather "The unlived life is not worth examining." The Polsters said "What is, is; and one thing follows another." Phenomenology asserts that while what we perceive is colored by our preconceptions and our method of viewing, we can learn to pay close attention to the actuality of our sensing, to what our senses tell us. We can also learn to recognize what preconceptions we bring to a situation, and to bracket them off, and thus come closer to an ability to relate to our environment in an immediate way. Notice the similarity to the 'awareness continuum' in Gestalt therapy.

There is also no dualism in Gestalt between 'mind' and 'body': There is no experience without body. This links with the existentialism of Merleau-Ponty (1962), who talked about the 'lived body' as the basis for experience.

The phenomenological grounding in the 'given' of body experience and fleeting awarenesses of environmental possibilities (what PHG calls 'id') forms the basis for the contacting and meaning-making processes which I shall now discuss.

FIGURE-GROUND

The ego functions of identification and alienation help us to do more than define self and other. They are the processes of creative adjustment in themselves. Out of the 'given'/'id,' I identify in the environment what is interesting, novel, or needful to me — make it figure — and alienate what is not of present interest to me — make it ground. That is, when we talk about ego functions, we are talking about figure/ground formation: The two are different formulations of the same act. Other names given in Gestalt theory to the same process are: Awareness; choice; creative adjustment; aggression; response-ability; and contact /with-drawal. These are all aspects of the same process.*

Notice that this process, however it's named, is not an 'internal' or 'mental' one, nor necessarily verbalized, but a process of orientation and action in the field, involving interaction, movement and communication as well as sensation and emotion. While we can separate these, and think about what we are doing before doing it, they are not inherently separate. Some situations are sufficiently complex, and our choices sufficiently crucial that we need to stop and think before we act. This stopping and thinking reduces the liveliness of our contact with the environment, but in some cases (e.g. situations where I want to negotiate diplomatically with some powerful other) I am quite glad to avoid some of the potential liveliness! The separation we then make is an interruption to the contact process (called 'egotism') in the service of making more effective contact in a complex situation.

This is covered in more depth in chapter 3, on 'creative adjustment.'

DIALOGIC THERAPY

The basis in Gestalt therapy for the dialogic method is that Gestalt field theory is inherently dialogic: The therapist and the client are co-creating each other in their contact. The dialogue

---

*I am aware that subtle distinctions can be made between these concepts (I want to thank Gary Yontef for pointing this out to me). For myself, I believe that more is lost than gained by emphasizing these distinctions. For example, 'awareness' tends to become merely a matter of perception, to distinguish it from 'contacting.' But in various parts of the literature, they are both identified with the process of making figures and grounds, i.e. gestalt formation.

Anyway, to say that they are all aspects of the same process (ego-functioning) is simpler, and, among all the complexities of Gestalt theory, any simplification which is not also a falsification is to be welcomed!

points to the field, rather than to the individuals. Thus the therapist provides an other in relation to which the client explores self. This is a particular kind of dialogue, not limited to verbal exchanges, but to the whole way in which we act towards each other and expect each other to act towards us. Questions in this dialogue are: How is the client presenting herself to me; and how is the client encouraging, or discouraging, me to present myself to her? With what characteristics is the client identifying — "This is what I am like." (what PHG calls 'personality function')? If the client brings an issue, dream, memory, what is the importance of that here and now, and what is she wanting from me in telling me? What am I wanting here, which parts of this are valid parts of the therapy, and which are guided by the client's expectations? Going back to the discussion of the principles of field theory, the dialogue is an example of the 'principle of singularity': A creation of unique people in an unique field.

EXPERIMENT

The other in relation to which I am self is not just other people. By the 'principle of possible relevance' discussed in chapter 2, it also includes my whole environment, including the inanimate objects round me; and also aspects of my functioning which I am presently disowning and making other. In Gestalt experiments, I can explore how I relate to these aspects of other, and try out new ways of relating. Thus in relation to the inanimate environment, I can explore my use of my senses: Looking, touching, smelling. Or I can explore my preferences: I like this, not that, or this aspect and not that aspect, or this is my emotional response to this environment. In relation to a disowned aspect of my functioning, I can dialogue— the famous Gestalt 'empty chair.' The aim is to create a 'safe emergency': A safe place where I can accept the anxiety of moving out of the familiar and risk acting differently.

Of course, in offering an experiment to a client, I am also engaging in dialogue in the sense that I was discussing above. In configuring myself as the provider of experiments, I am encouraging the client to configure himself as someone who takes my advice. I therefore need to decide whether, with a particular client, I regard this as worthwhile. For example, with a compliant client, I will be very careful not to offer experiments, because I would expect the client to do them for me, rather than asking himself whether he is interested and willing to do what I ask. My rule of thumb is that I do not introduce experiments unless and until I have good evidence of the client's willingness to say 'no' to me, even/especially if the client wants me to tell him what to do.

With a client who habitually says 'no,' it may become an experiment in itself for the client to risk accepting my suggestions, and configuring me as someone with authority who is also safe and on the client's side. I must particularly in this situation not be invested in any particular outcome, and as ready to explore the process by which the client says 'no,' as to exploring the consequences of saying 'yes.'

The important factor here as elsewhere is the paradoxical theory of change. The aim of the experiment is not to encourage the client to end up acting differently. Rather the aim is to invite them to move out of confluence with a particular way of being, so that way of being, and its alternatives, become available to awareness. The distinction I am pointing to is between the client's aware acceptance of where he is, and his confluence with where he is, so that no awareness is possible.

Chapter 9 looks at 'dialogue and experiment,' and the relationship between them, in more detail.

INTERRUPTIONS TO CONTACT

It is part of our basic human ability to transcend the situation in which we find ourselves that we are able to interrupt the contacting process if we find it too anxiety-producing, or not to our liking. Some commentators have taken Gestalt theory to say that the 'interruptions' are bad in themselves, and either agree with this, or offer various 'reinterpretations' of Gestalt that make them OK, or stop calling them 'interruptions.' But it is clear from PHG that the basis of neurosis is not interruption of contact, but loss of ego functions, that is loss of ownership and choicefulness of the process of contacting or interrupting. I reach a particular point and there is a jarring as I move away from a particular kind of contact without making figural that I am doing it. PHG talks about the autonomous criterion of experience: Whatever the content of my experience, is the figure I form bright, clear, graceful, unified, etc.? If not, if it is dull, confused, or energyless, then something in the environment or in my needs is being avoided, and the ground is demanding energy from the figure.

A further point which is often lost is that Gestalt is a therapy which emphasizes non-confluence between therapist and client. Thus we are able to configure our interaction in different ways. The client can interrupt contact, and the therapist not be interrupted — since phenomenologically the therapist does not require any particular contact, but relates with interest to what the client does do.*

THE CYCLE OF AWARENESS

I have explained in Chapter 3 my view that this theoretical concept does not fit with the Gestalt theory I am presenting here, but it does fit with what happens with our awareness if we add

---

*In the same way, Wheeler and others' emphasis on 'structure of ground' assumes that what is figure for client is figure for therapist, and what is ground for client is ground for therapist, i.e. confluence! I can't pay attention to ground— it becomes figure if I do. But what is figure for me is not necessarily, and often isn't, figure for client.

delay, thinking and planning (what PHG call 'egotism') to our relating. Then the unified activity of sensation/awareness/mobilization of energy/action to final contact becomes split and sequential: This is the aim of egotism, to delay the action in a difficult environment, where we want to try things out in fantasy before living it out in the world.

PHG has its own cycle: Forecontact: the given/id; contacting: ego/making figure and ground; final contact: total engagement in a clear figure, no interest in ground; and post contact: moving back to id. Each of these involves a different level of sensing, awareness, energization, action and contacting. Each aspect is relational, as opposed to the Zinker cycle, where much is intrapsychic. It is thus a superficially similar theory, but is actually quite different in its underlying assumptions and philosophy.

THE LAYERS OF NEUROSIS

This fits much better into the map. The 'impasse' is where we take the existential risk of moving beyond our identifications/'personality function'/'role playing layer,' and experience the anxiety inherent in doing so. The 'implosion' is the move from loss of ego functions, and thus the simplicities of 'doing what I always do,' to the facing of the existential question "What do I choose" and the risk of putting myself on the line. At first I am lost, with no external signposts and nowhere for my energy to go (the 'implosion'), then I choose, direct my energy, and 'explode' with unity, color and grace (the autonomous criterion). Looked at from this perspective, it is clear that the place of Gestalt experiments is in moving beyond the role-playing personality to awareness of loss of ego functions, and thus the impasse. It is interesting also from this perspective that Erv Polster's new book *A Population of Selves* is geared towards a redefinition of Gestalt therapy as a therapy of the role-playing layer rather than of the existential impasse (see Philippson, 1996).

CONCLUSION

I hope this discussion of the way the different strands of Gestalt theory fit together, and arise out of Gestalt field theory, forms a useful 'map' of the Gestalt landscape. I am aware that it is one of many possible maps, and that different Gestalt theorists draw the map in different ways. My hope would be that each of these maps could be elaborated (as Polster has done), so that a dialogue between clear figures becomes possible. My hope also is that those who teach and learn Gestalt therapy give attention to the overall map of their own approach, so that the interrelations between the various terms they use are clear rather than the terms being fragmented.

I have attempted in this book to present a coherent, and philosophically cogent, account of Gestalt therapy. I have found it a difficult task: I find that doing it in practice (both as therapist and as client) shows the approach much more clearly than words on paper can. No words can replace experience! I hope, however, that something of my understanding of Gestalt has come through to you, the reader. With my interest in dialogue, I hope I can get some feedback.

I am also aware of how my understanding of Gestalt therapy has developed, and continues to develop. No statement of the theory can or should be final, and I am sure that I would have said some things differently if I were writing at a later time. I hope that more debate on theory develops, and I am heartened by the growing number of journals internationally that are dedicated to Gestalt therapy.

As I look back over what I have written, which is a restatement of themes from PHG, I am amazed at the insight involved in distilling such a coherent approach from such a variety of influences by such strong and varied personalities. I present regularly on 'Gestalt as a therapy of relational self' to both Gestalt and non-

Gestalt audiences, usually experientially, sometimes by showing a videotape, and enjoy participants' surprise at the power and vigor of the approach. I have developed a faith that something will emerge from even comparatively short experiences of this work. I hope I have managed to communicate some of my excitement and trust in this way of working.

Chapter 15

WRITING FROM A CLIENT —
A CLIENT'S VIEW OF THERAPY

Peter says to write about how it has been for me to have changed from being so split to being mostly one. I'm not used to writing about myself in this way unless I address my words to Peter because we all seem to trust him and it helps us to think more clearly.

So,

Dear Peter,

I've been in therapy with you for about ten years now, and in all that time I haven't changed. I am still the woman that my partner loves. And, at the same time, I am entirely changed. I am no longer a robot who responds automatically to every situation she encounters. I can recognize my feelings and choose how I would like to respond. Living is more confusing and more painful and, I am happy to say, more joyful.

I remember when I first came to see you and we talked about the enormous lie I had told my friends. The one about having been violently raped in a park when actually I had been merely harassed by a youth of about fourteen years old. The boy's harassing me, with its overtly sexual overtones, had so shaken me that I felt as if I had indeed been violently sexually assaulted. I needed to tell a story that would be able to express how I felt. I couldn't have told the truth because no one would have understood the state of shock I was in, the deep distress and disorientation I was feeling, the intense fear I was experiencing. Nothing in the present had happened to me that could explain the intensity of my reaction.

My world was like this before I came to see you. I was constantly triggered into feeling emotions that were entirely out of synch with my present. I would frequently see things that weren't there, I would often say things that weren't what I thought I was thinking. I would know about things that I didn't know I had ever experienced or learned. For example, when I was about thirteen, I talked with my high school science teacher about men's steam baths and what went on in them. I know that he didn't want to believe that I had been in one, but I was also expressing knowledge that I couldn't have known if I hadn't experienced it first hand. We were both confused. I felt as if I had been lying. I didn't know how I knew what I knew but I was confident that I was right, and I could tell from his reaction that I had indeed been accurate about the details.

This is what it meant to me to be split within myself. I kept trying to persuade myself that I was normal, that I couldn't be so different from other people. Now I understand my experience differently. I know that sometimes there is another part of myself feeling and/or speaking to you. I have come to understand that others of me are speaking and feeling and remembering, and that at the same time I am still me.

So much of me, or should I say, so many of us, had been locked away for so long. I think that some of me wasn't born yet because I had been abused since birth. I remember a session with you when I felt what it was to be clean and pure and virginal. It is an experience I had never known before, ever. It wasn't a part of me that had been lost. Rather, I felt as if that part of me hadn't existed until that session. You and I are finding myselves and I am now becoming a whole instead of pieces. My mental pictures of myself constantly change. Often I have had to bring together several parts of a part of me just to form one piece of the frag-mented mirror. For example, the part of me that has had to deal with so many details of death is also fragmented. She has one part to deal with freezing to death, another to deal with dismember-ment, another for burial and so on. And, it seems to me that different parts of my personality, my ability to feel or understand something, was locked away with those parts of her.

Now that I have a lot of me back I have a much greater range of experience. I am less paranoid, less defensive, less self-destruct-ive. I am more able to respond to a situation with an appropriate emotion. For example, my work as a teacher has always been based on the building of relationships with my students. In the past, I would be confused by their ordinary adolescent behavior and I would seek to control what I didn't understand. Now, as I have found the lost adolescents within myself, I am able to appreciate the pressures my students are under, and what their needs are in terms of me, as an adult. I am more distant from them, more respectful of the process that they are going through in attempting to define themselves. I could never have under-stood that before I came to see you. I had a rigid, robotic, unyielding definition of myself that I thought was me. I had never undergone adolescence with all the questions of who am I and who do I want to be? Somehow that had been determined long ago, in early childhood by me, by others who were molding me, creating me in their image.

The point is, that ten years ago I was unable to experience empathy for others because I had missed out on experiences that were common to other people. Essential parts of myself had been left to fend for themselves, entirely out of my awareness. They could not be reached. I didn't even know that they were there. But, you and I reached them in therapy. You, in particular, recognized them and listened and even reached out to them, to me, when they made an appearance. We felt seen by you. We felt able to be ourselves. If we couldn't speak, then you listened in other ways. If we couldn't be making sense then you let us not make sense and did your best. That was enough.

You taught me to do that. You showed me how to listen to myselves. It's almost that simple. So now when somebody inside expresses a feeling that is out of synch with the present or says words that do not fit with what is happening, I know how to listen to her. I know that she has something valuable to offer at that moment and that she is actually a part of me. Gradually, I am beginning to not have to speak to myself in that way. Gradually, we are becoming a part of the woman we all are. I am beginning to know myself without having to refer to myselves to find out what I want, what I need to know, who I am, what it is I am going to do.

I am glad that I have been lucky enough to have both you and John as therapists. Together you have provided me with the opportunities to come alive. There are parts of me that will not speak to you but speak easily to John. We have had the luxury of being able to keep one of you for ourselves if the other was projected on to, or was part of an ugly transference on our part that would keep us distant. Someone could be hating you but keep John as her friend, or be afraid of John and keep you as her confidant. I know that you two talk to each other about my process, and that has provided the safety net. The important thing is that we always have somebody on our side. This is essential because I don't think that I have always been on my own side.

I think that it is significant that I have two male therapists. It would have been impossible for me to make the progress I have if I had been working with a woman. I would have been too close to terror to work. I couldn't have trusted or, to begin with, even respected her. However, one day we would like to work with a woman therapist. It's frightening to even contemplate but if we are to be whole then it will be necessary. After all, we are a woman. I am glad that I am now able to make women friends and enjoy their company. I have begun to learn what it is to be a girl. I like talking with girls and women. I am beginning to have something in common with them. We, who were so damaged by our mother, are beginning to understand that she was not indicative of all women. Our mother, female psychopath, is unusual in her extremity. Her self-hatred is belonging to her and is no longer ours. We are separating from her. Because of this, I can live as I choose and not who she would have had me be.

So, I am striving to be myself and I think that I am succeeding. I used to feel that I was many individuals contained in one body. Now I feel whole and contained as one individual with different parts. For me there is a vast difference in these two perceptions of myself. I am changing so quickly that I know that if I read this again in a year, what I have written will still be true but will seem incomplete. I suspect that by then my language will have changed and perhaps it will not be "we" who would write to you but "me."

As always, Peter, thanks for listening.

REFERENCES

Bateson, Jackson, Haley & Weakland (1972) "Towards a theory of schizophrenia" in Bateson (ed.) *Steps to an Ecology of Mind*. Ballantine Books, New York.

Coveney, P. & Highfield, R. (1991) *The Arrow of Time*. Flamingo, London.

Crocker, S.F. (1981) "Proflection." *The Gestalt Journal*, Vol. 4, No. 2. Highland, NY.

Dossey, L. (1982) *Space, Time and Medicine*. Shambhala, Boulder.

DSM-IV (1994) *The Diagnostic and Statistical Manual of Mental Disorders*. American Psychiatric Association.

Enright, J. (1970) "An Introduction to Gestalt Techniques ." In Fagan & Shepherd (op. cit.)

Erickson, M.H. (1980) *The Collected Works of Milton H. Erickson on Hypnosis*. (4 volumes) Ed. E.L. Rossi. Irvington, New York.

Fagan & Shepherd (eds.) (1970) *Gestalt Therapy Now: Theory, Techniques, Applications.* Science and Behavior Books: Palo Alto, CA.

Friedlaender, S. (1918) *Schopferische Indifferenz.* Georg Muller, Munich.

Friedman, M. (1990) "Dialogue, Philosophical Anthropology, and Gestalt Therapy." *The Gestalt Journal*, Vol. XIII, No. 1, Highland, NY.

From, I. (1984) "Reflections on Gestalt Therapy after Thirty-two Years of Practice: A Requiem for Gestalt." *The Gestalt Journal* Vol. VII No. 1, Highland, NY.

Gell-Mann, M. (1994) *The Quark and the Jaguar.* Little, Brown, London.

Gleick, J. (1987) *Chaos: Making a New Science.* Viking Press, New York.

Goldstein, K. (1939) *The Organism.* American Book Company, Boston.

Greenberg, E. (1989) "Healing the Borderline." *The Gestalt Journal* Vol. XII No. 2, Highland, NY.

Greenberg, E. (1991) *Special: The Diagnosis and Treatment of Narcissistic Disorders.* Gestalt Center of Long Island 14th Annual Conference Presentation.

Haley, J. (ed.) (1971) *Changing Families.* Grune & Stratton, New York.

Harris, J. (1996) "Silence in Groups." *British Gestalt Journal* Vol. 5 No. 1

Hill, R.B. (1979) *Hanta Yo.* Futura, London.

Kernberg, O. (1975) *Borderline Conditions and Pathological Narcissism.* Science House, New York.

Kirschenbaum, H. & Henderson, V.L. (eds.) (1990) *Carl Rogers Dialogues.* Constable, London.

Kohut, H. (1977) *The Restoration of the Self.* International University Press, New York.

Kuhn, T. (1970) *The Structure of Scientific Revolutions.* University of Chicago Press, Chicago.

Land, E. (1977) "The Retinex Theory of Colour Vision." *Scientific American,* Dec. 1977.

Lasch, C. 1979 *The Culture of Narcissism.* Norton/Abacus, London.

Latner, J. (1983) "This is the speed of light: field and systems theories in Gestalt therapy." *The Gestalt Journal* Vol. VI No. 2, Highland, NY. Also the debate on Latner's paper and Gestalt theory taking up the whole of *The Gestalt Journal* Vol. VII No. 1 (Spring 1984).

Latner, J. 1986 *The Gestalt Therapy Book.* The Gestalt Journal Press, Highland, NY.

Lao Tse (1972) *Tao Te Ching.* Tr. Feng, G. & English, J. Wildwood House, London.

Mahler, J.S., Pine, F., Bergman, A. (1975) *The Psychological Birth of the Human Infant.* Basic Books, New York.

Maslow, A. (1968) *Toward a Psychology of Being.* Van Nostrand, New York

Masterson, J.F. (1981) *The Narcissistic and Borderline Disorders.* Brunner Mazel, New York.

Merleau-Ponty, M. (1962) *Phenomenology of Perception.* (C Smith, trans.). Routledge & Kegan Paul, London.

Palazzoli, M.S., Boscolo, L., Cecchin, G. & Prata, G. (1978) *Paradox and Counter-Paradox.* Jason Aronson, New York.

Parlett, M. (1991). "Reflections on Field Theory ." *British Gestalt Journal*, Vol. 1, No. 2.

Peat, F.D. (1994) *Blackfoot Physics.* Fourth Estate, London.

Perls, F.S. (1947) *Ego, Hunger and Aggression.* Allen Unwin, London.

Perls, F.S. (1948) "Theory and Technique of Personality Integration." *American Journal of Psychotherapy*, Vol. 2 No. 4 (Oct. 1948), reprinted in Stevens (1975).

Perls, F., Hefferline, R., Goodman, P. (1994/1951) *Gestalt Therapy: Excitement and Growth in the Human Personality.* The Gestalt Journal Press, New York.

Perls, F.S. (1978) "Finding Self through Gestalt Therapy," in *The Gestalt Journal* Vol. I No. 1 (Winter 1978), Highland, NY.

Perls, F.S. (1969) *Gestalt Therapy Verbatim.* Real People Press, Moab.

Perls, F.S. (1973) *The Gestalt Approach and Eye Witness to Therapy.* Bantam Books, New York.

Philippson, P.A. (1990) "Awareness, the Contact Boundary and the Field." *The Gestalt Journal* Vol. XIII No. 2, Highland, NY.

Philippson, P.A. (1991) "Gestalt Reconsidered Again." *British Gestalt Journal* Vol. 1 No. 2.

Philippson, P.A. (1995) "Two Theories of Five Layers." *Topics in Gestalt Therapy*, Vol. 3. No. 1, Manchester.

Philippson, P. (1996) A Population of Gestalt Therapies: a Review of Erv Polster's *A Population of Selves. British Gestalt Journal*

Philippson, P. & Harris, J. (1992) *Gestalt: Working with Groups.* Manchester Gestalt Centre.

Polster, E. & M. (1973) *Gestalt Therapy Integrated.* Brunner Mazel, New York.

Resnick, R. (1995) "Gestalt Therapy: Principles, Prisms and Perspectives." *British Gestalt Journal*, Vol. 4, No. 1

Rogers, C. (1951) *Client Centered Therapy.* Houghton Mifflin

Rossi, E.L. (1986) *The Psychobiology of Mind-Body Healing.* Norton, New York.

Smith, E. (ed.) (1977) *The Growing Edge of Gestalt Therapy.* Citadel Press, Secaucus, NJ.

Smuts, J. (1996) *Holism and Evolution.* Gestalt Journal Press, Highland, NY. First published 1925

Stern, D. (1985) *The Interpersonal World of the Infant.* Basic Books, New York.

Stevens, J. (1975) *Gestalt Is.* Real People's Press, Moab.

Stolorow, R., Atwood, G. & Brandchaft, B. (1994) *The Intersubjective Perspective.* Jason Aaronson Inc., Northvale, NJ.

Tobin, S. (1982) "Self-Disorders, Gestalt Therapy and Self Psychology." *The Gestalt Journal* Vol. V No. 2, Highland, NY.

Waldrop, M.M. (1993) *Complexity.* Viking Press, London.

Ward, C. (1993). *Fringe Benefits.* New Statesman and Society, London, 17/31 Dec. 1993.

Wheeler, G. (1991) *Gestalt Reconsidered.* Gestalt Institute of Cleveland Press, Cleveland.

Yontef, G. (1988) "Assimilating Diagnostic and Psychoanalytic Perspectives into Gestalt Therapy." *The Gestalt Journal* Vol. XI No. 1, Highland, NY.

Zinker, J. (1977) *Creative Process in Gestalt Therapy.* Vintage Books, New York.

Zinker, J. (1994) *In Search of Good Form.* Jossey-Bass, San Francisco.

Zohar, D. (1991) *The Quantum Self.* Flamingo, London.

INDEX

Join the Gestalt Journal Press On-Line Book Club

Send your email address to <club@gestalt.org> with "join" as the subject and receive a special promotion code that will give you a 15% discount at the online store with the most comprehensive selection of books, CDs, & DVDs relating to the theory and practice of Gestalt therapy available anywhere.
www.gjpstore.com

Explore the world of Gestalt therapy online and locate a Gestalt therapist in the International Guide to Gestalt Practitioners at
www.gestalttherapy.net

For a complete, up-to-date calendar of Gestalt therapy workshops, training events and conferences read *Gestalt News and Notes*
at
www.gestalt.org/news